AFP World News Report 6

AFPニュースで見る世界 6

Makoto Shishido

Kevin Murphy

Mariko Takahashi

SEIBIDO

photographs by
Alamy Stock Photo / iStockPhoto
DVD / Streaming Materials

LESSON 1: ©JAN FLEMR / AFPTV / AFP
LESSON 2: ©JONATHAN KLEIN / AFPTV / AFP
LESSON 3: ©WILLIAM EDWARDS, ARMAN SOLDIN, GLYN KIRK / AFPTV / AFP
LESSON 4: ©ELEONORE SENS, KATIE SCHUBAUER / AFPTV / AFP
LESSON 5: ©ELODIE LE MAOU, KATHERINE LEVY SPENCER / AFPTV / AFP
LESSON 6: ©JORDI PERDIGO / AFPTV / AFP
LESSON 7: ©JONATHAN KLEIN, SIPPACHAI KUNNU-WONG / AFPTV / AFP
LESSON 8: ©WILLIAM EDWARDS / AFPTV / AFP
LESSON 9: ©SELIM CHTAYTI, ARNAUD RICHARD / AFPTV / AFP
LESSON 10: ©KATIE SCHUBAUER, AGNES BUN / AFPTV / AFP

LESSON 11: ©MATHILDE BELLENGER / AFPTV / AFP
LESSON 12: ©ROBERTO SCHMIDT, GIANRIGO MAR-LETTA, VIRGINIE GOUBIER, HANDOUT, AGNES BUN, SAUL LOEB, DEBORAH BLOOM, TAMI CHAPPELL / AFP / COURTESY OF KAMALA HARRIS / AFPTV / DC POOL / TWITTER / @KAMALAHARRIS / UNITED STATES SENATE
LESSON 13: ©VOLANA RAZAFIMANANTSOA / AFPTV / AFP
LESSON 14: ©TOM LITTLE, JONATHAN NACKSTRAND / AFPTV / AFP
LESSON 15: ©KATIE SCHUBAUER / AFPTV / AFP
LESSON 16: ©TOM LITTLE / AFPTV / NATIONAL MARITIME AND TRANSPORT MUSEUM OF SWEDEN / AFP

StreamLine

Web 動画・音声ファイルのストリーミング再生について

CD マーク及び Web 動画マークがある箇所は、PC、スマートフォン、タブレット端末において、無料でストリーミング再生することができます。下記 URL よりご利用ください。再生手順や動作環境などは本書巻末の「Web 動画のご案内」をご覧ください。

https://st.seibido.co.jp

音声ファイルのダウンロードについて

CD マークがある箇所は、ダウンロードすることも可能です。下記 URL の書籍詳細ページにあるダウンロードアイコンをクリックしてください。

https://seibido.co.jp/ad643

AFP World News Report 6

LINGUAPORTA

> ## リンガポルタ連動テキストをご購入の学生さんは、「リンガポルタ」を無料でご利用いただけます！

　本テキストで学習していただく内容に準拠した問題を、オンライン学習システム「リンガポルタ」で学習していただくことができます。PCだけでなく、スマートフォンやタブレットでも学習できます。単語や文法、リスニング力などをよりしっかり身に付けていただくため、ぜひ積極的に活用してください。

　リンガポルタの利用にはアカウントとアクセスコードの登録が必要です。登録方法については下記ページにアクセスしてください。

https://www.seibido.co.jp/linguaporta/register.html

本テキスト「AFP World News Report 6」のアクセスコードは下記です。

7250-2046-1231-0365-0003-0073-23VZ-NCV6

・リンガポルタの学習機能（画像はサンプルです。また、すべてのテキストに以下の4つの機能が用意されているわけではありません）

● 多肢選択

● 空所補充（音声を使っての聞き取り問題も可能）

● 単語並びかえ（マウスや手で単語を移動）

● マッチング（マウスや手で単語を移動）

3

はじめに

　本書は、AFP-World Academic Archive の映像ニュースで取り上げられた、世界中で起こるさまざまな最新の話題に触れながら、初中級レベルの英語力を養成することを目的としています。英語を聞き、理解する力、英文を読み、内容を理解する力、各課のテーマについて自らの意見を考え、発表をする力を養成するために必要と考える練習問題を、さまざまな工夫を凝らし、配列しています。利用する学生が興味を引くような、身近な社会の話題について、AFP のニュース映像と、読みやすい英文を利用し、基礎的な英語理解力を高めるとともに、英語を聴く力、読む力、意見を述べる力を養成することを主眼とした、初中級者向けの教材です。

　本書の構成は下記のような特徴を持っています。

1. **Listening** は、AFP WAA のニュース映像を各課の話題への導入として利用しています。学生に各課のテーマについて興味を持たせる役割を持っています。

　　1. **Key Word Study** は、ニュース映像に出てくる基礎的な重要単語を学ぶことで、話題への理解と単語力の強化を目指します。
　　2. **Listening Practice − First Viewing** は、ニュース映像の全体像を理解するための T/F 形式の問題です。
　　3. **Listening Practice 2** は、細かな音の聞き取りを確認するディクテーションの問題です。
　　4. **Comprehension Check − Second Viewing** は、さらに詳細な内容を理解しているか確認するための練習問題です。
　　5. **Summary** は、映像で紹介されたニュースの要旨を理解しているか、最終的に確認する問題です。音声を聞き、空所を補充する形式となっています。

2. **Reading** は、英文読解を通じて各課のニュース映像で紹介された問題事例の内容を展開させ、さまざまな意見を紹介するものです。この英文は中心となる話題や意見の提示で、比較的容易に英語で書かれた 260 〜 280 語程度の英文読解です。現代社会で話題となっている諸問題に関する情報を読むばかりでなく、基本的な英語力、単語力、読解力、思考力を身につけることを目指しています。

　　1. **Vocabulary Check** は、英文の中で取り上げられている基礎的な英単語の学習です。
　　2. **Comprehension Questions** は、英文の内容理解を問う問題です。学生が自ら英語で答える形式の問になっています。
　　3. **Grammar Check** は、基本的な文法事項の確認を兼ねた語順整序演習です。

3. **Discussion** では、学生が積極的に参加する対話型講義への展開として、批判的思考に基づいた学生の意見を発表させることを目指しております。各課で提示される話題に関して、対立する 2 つの主張について自らの意見をまとめ、個々の学生による発表、グループごとの発表、ディベート形式での討論など指導者の裁量でさまざまな展開が可能であると考えます。

　以上 3 部のさまざまな練習問題から、現代社会で話題となっている事柄について英語で考えながら、単語力、聴解力、読解力、文法理解力、発話力、討論力など総合的な英語能力の養成に役立つでしょう。本書を活用し、英語力の一層の向上と、社会におけるさまざまな最新情報に対する正しい理解が図られ、健全な社会生活を送るための一助となることを願います。

　なお、スクリプト、英文の注釈等には細心の注意を払って作成いたしましたが、お気づきの点がございましたらご教授いただければ幸いです。

　最後になりましたが、本書の編集、出版にあたり、ひとかたならぬご尽力を賜った㈱成美堂、萩原美奈子氏に心より感謝申し上げます。

2021 年 9 月

著者一同

CONTENTS

Natural vs Artificial:
For AI voice assistance

科学技術が進歩し、人工音声が多く利用されています。スマートスピーカーやスマホの音声ガイドなど、機械が人に話しかけるようになりました。一方では人工音声に違和感を覚える人もいるようです。人間の声と人工音声どちらの音声を好むか議論しましょう。

I LISTENING

1 KEY WORD STUDY | *Before Watching the Video*

▷▷ *Match each word with its definition.*

1. diagnosis	( )	2. ideally	( )	3. mobile	( )
4. procedure	( )	5. provide	( )	6. statistical	( )
7. surgery	( )	8. swift	( )	9. synthetic	( )
10. undergo	( )				

a. 手段	b. 提供する	c. 診断	d. 手術
e. 経験する	f. 統計の	g. 理想的に	h. 迅速な
i. 合成の	j. 携帯の		

2 LISTENING PRACTICE 1 | *First Viewing* (Time 01:53) 🖥 WEB動画 💿 DVD

▷▷ *Watch the news clip and write T if the statement is true or F if it is false.*

1. Vlastimil Gular lost his voice after undergoing surgery for lung cancer
   a year ago. ( )
2. Jindrich Matousek uses statistical models to create synthetic speech. ( )
3. Jana Huttova would like her small children to still hear a robotic voice. ( )
4. Vlastimil Gular did not record any sentences before having his larynx
   removed. ( )
5. Vlastimil Gular provided enough input information to produce a voice. ( )

9

WEB動画 DVD CD 1-03

▷▷ *Listen to the recording and fill in the missing words.*

Narrator: Vlastimil Gular lost his voice after undergoing surgery for throat cancer a year ago. But thanks to a high-tech app spearheaded by two Czech universities, ¹( ) ( ) ( ) ( ) ( ) ( ).

spearhead 先頭に立つ

Jindrich Matousek: Our project is unique in that we are trying to create a tailor-made synthetic voice for each user.

Narrator: The app was developed for people who are set to lose their voice due to a laryngectomy, or removal of the larynx, a typical procedure for throat cancer. ²( ) ( ) ( ), scientists first record the patient reading as many sentences as possible. Then they use statistical models to create synthetic speech that can be played on the patients' mobile phones or tablets via the app. Jana is in the process of recording her voice ahead of a minor operation on her throat.

laryngectomy 喉頭摘出術

larynx 喉頭

Jana Huttova: If I have a problem and ³( ) ( ) ( ) ( ) ( ) ( ), I would like my small children to still hear my voice, not a robotic one.

Narrator: Ideally, patients need to record more than 10,000 sentences to provide scientists with enough material to produce their synthetic voice. But cancer often demands swift treatment, ⁴( ) ( ) ( ) ( ) ( ) ( ) to do recordings.

Barbora Repova: It's often a matter of weeks, three at the most, during which you can record the voice.

Narrator: Vlastimil managed to record only 477 sentences before having his larynx removed.

Vlastímil Gular: I underwent total laryngectomy within 23 days of diagnosis.

Narrator: But even this paltry input provided enough information to produce a voice ⁵(   )

(   ) (   )

(   ) (   )

(   ).

paltry わずかな

-----

4 | COMPREHENSION CHECK | *Second Viewing*

WEB動画 DVD

▷▷ *Watch the news clip again and answer the following questions in English.*

1. In what aspect is Jindrich Matousek's project unique?

    ....

2. For what people was the app developed?

    ....

3. Ideally, how many sentences do patients need to record to provide scientists with enough material to produce their synthetic voice?

    ....

4. How many weeks at the most does it take to record the patient's voice?

    ....

5. How many days after his diagnosis did Vlastimil Gular undergo a total laryngectomy?

    ....

5 | SUMMARY

CD 1-04

▷▷ *Listen to the recording and complete the summary.*

Vlastimil Gular lost his voice after undergoing surgery for throat cancer a year ago. The app was ¹(   ) for people who are set to lose their voice due to a laryngectomy, a typical procedure for throat cancer. Ideally, patients need to record

11

more than 10,000 sentences to ²(   ) scientists with enough material to produce their synthetic voice. Vlastimil managed to record only 477 sentences before having his larynx removed. But even this paltry input provided enough ³(   ) to produce a voice that he can call his own.

▌▌ READING

🎴 1-05

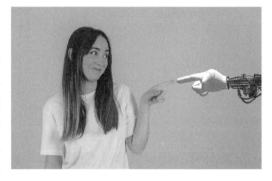

Since the 1990s, progress in voice-based technology is transforming daily life. Voice-recognition software, whether on wearable devices such as watches or found
5　in gadgets such as Siri or Alexa, is a growing feature of the modern world. It is now used, for example, to access information, create smart homes, or control media. Moreover, Automatic Speech Recognition (ASR) software now allows a computer to
10　respond as a human might. ASR can be life-changing for people with visual or voice impairments. The subtitles or text it produces can allow the physically challenged to better deal with the world around them. The advantages of this technology are undeniable. Those who have lost their power of speech or have difficulty with it can regain control over their lives. Companies can use unique voices for marketing and
15　customer interaction, and businesses can increase productivity using voice-activated commands.

However, although voice technology has many advantages in health, the home, or business, there are concerns. There are worries about the ethics, security, and privacy of such devices. One problem is that robots are sounding too much like humans.
20　Applications are available that can closely mimic the sound of a real voice. Is a conversation ethical if a person does not know they are communicating with a robot? Robots may record the data and allow others to use it in a harmful way. Furthermore, a device that may always be listening causes many people to feel nervous. Data collected in this way may be sold or used to commit fraud.
25　Authentic voice technology will make real changes to many lives, but companies must address concerns over the implications of using such technology and how data will be collected and managed.

(282 words)

▌NOTES

impairment 障がい　　**fraud** 詐欺

1 VOCABULARY CHECK

▷▷ *Fill in the blanks with the most appropriate word from the list below.*

1. New (   ) are introduced to the market every year.
2. It is still too early to assess the (   ) of the study.
3. You need to (   ) your account first in order to shop on this website.
4. It is (   ) that technology has changed our lives.
5. The use of (   ) materials is essential for learning a new language.

> undeniable   authentic   implications   gadgets   activate

2 COMPREHENSION QUESTIONS

▷▷ *Answer the following questions in English.*

1. For what purposes is voice-recognition software used?

    ....

2. What does ASR stand for?

    ....

3. Who are likely to benefit the most from ASR?

    ....

4. What is a problem of robots sounding too much like humans?

    ....

5. What is a potential risk of devices collecting data?

    ....

3 GRAMMAR CHECK

▷▷ *Unscramble the following words and complete the sentences.*

1. Some people [relationships, difficulty, interpersonal, have, with] at their workplace.

    Some people .... at their workplace.

2. The management team [situation, the, able, with, was, to, deal] promptly.

    The management team .... promptly.

3. Self-driving cars will [drive, allow, more, before, people, than, safely, to].

    Self-driving cars will ....

III DISCUSSION

Natural vs Artificial: For AI voice assistance

There are many AI voice assistant devices such as Siri, smart speakers, and GPS.
What kind of voice would you prefer to listen to?

▷▷ インターネットなどを利用し、人工音声について調べましょう。人工音声の発展や今後の可能性など良い点ばかりでなく、人間の聴覚や思考への影響など悪い点についても検討し、下記のどちらの意見を支持するか、主張、理由など自らの考えをまとめ、発表しましょう。

Which opinion do you support and why?

A *I would like AI voice assistant devices to use a natural-sounding human voice.*

B *I would not mind them using an artificial voice.*

自分の意見 ＿＿＿＿＿＿＿

理由

＿＿＿＿＿＿＿＿＿＿＿＿＿＿＿＿＿＿＿＿＿＿＿＿＿＿＿＿＿＿＿＿＿

＿＿＿＿＿＿＿＿＿＿＿＿＿＿＿＿＿＿＿＿＿＿＿＿＿＿＿＿＿＿＿＿＿

＿＿＿＿＿＿＿＿＿＿＿＿＿＿＿＿＿＿＿＿＿＿＿＿＿＿＿＿＿＿＿＿＿

＿＿＿＿＿＿＿＿＿＿＿＿＿＿＿＿＿＿＿＿＿＿＿＿＿＿＿＿＿＿＿＿＿

REFERENCES

A

『肉声と合成音声が脳波に与える影響の比較検討』大塚 敦夫・富山 健（研究報告知能システム (ICS) 2013-ICS-171(10), 1-3, 2013-03-11)
人工的あるいは非人間的な要素を持つ合成音声が人の感情にどのような影響を与えるのかを検証した研究。非人間的な特徴量を持つ合成音声は人間の感情に影響を与えると考えられることが分かった。

B

Google「Text-to-Speech」
テキストを自然な音声に変換できる。人間にかなり近い音声を実現。40 以上の言語と言語変種で 220 種類以上の音声から選択できる。

Relocating vs Protecting Buildings: How to preserve historical sites

地球温暖化の影響からか、海面上昇や浸食などの地形変化が各地で問題となっています。文化財を保存するためには移転や防波堤、保護壁の建設、かさ上げなどの方法が考えられます。どの方策が良いと思いますか。

▰ LISTENING

1 KEY WORD STUDY | *Before Watching the Video*

▷▷ *Match each word with its definition.*

1. affected	( )	2. Buddhist	( )	3. demarcation	( )
4. erode	( )	5. floating	( )	6. fragile	( )
7. inland	( )	8. monastery	( )	9. restore	( )
10. tide	( )				

a. 壊れやすい	b. 境界線	c. 潮流	d. 浮かんでいる
e. 仏教徒	f. 修復する	g. 修道院	h. 影響を受けた
i. 内陸	j. 浸食する		

2 LISTENING PRACTICE 1 | *First Viewing*   (Time 02:09) WEB動画 DVD

▷▷ *Watch the news clip and write T if the statement is true or F if it is false.*

1. The Buddhist temple in Thailand has been in the middle of the village for 30 years.   ( )
2. Some of the world's largest mangrove forests exist in the Gulf of Thailand.( )
3. Bangkok's border is about 2 km in the sea from where the people live.   ( )
4. The waves, tides, and currents in the Gulf of Thailand are higher than before.
                                                                              ( )
5. A mangrove forest is a symbol of Thailand's disappearing shores.   ( )

3 | LISTENING PRACTICE 2

 WEB動画 DVD CD 1-07

▷▷ *Listen to the recording and fill in the missing words.*

Narrator: Lost to the sea—just 30 years ago, this Buddhist temple in Thailand was in the middle of the village it served. But ¹( ) ( ) ( ) ( ) at a rate of nearly 30 meters every year along some parts of the coastline. The villagers fled years ago, rebuilding their homes several hundred meters inland. But the abbot is standing firm.

abbot 修道院長

Somnuek Atipanyo: If the temple were moved, people wouldn't know there used to be a temple here that was destroyed. But if we stay and ²( ) ( ) ( ), we can go on.

Narrator: The Gulf of Thailand boasts some of the world's largest mangrove forests. The mangrove roots used to hold together these shores, but swathes were cleared to make way for shrimp farms and salt production plants. A quarter of the Thai coastline—some 700 kilometers—is thought to be affected by coastal erosion. Now there's a push to try to restore the fragile ecosystem— ³( ) ( ) ( ) ( ) ( ) ( ) Bangkok to help re-plant the seawater forest.

The Gulf of Thailand タイ湾

swathe 帯状のもの[場所・土地]

Pongsak Ruangpatikorn: Bangkok's mangrove forest has been eroded. In fact, Bangkok's demarcation is now in the sea, some two kilometers in the sea from where the people live.

Narrator: Bamboo barriers and cement pylons are also being used to shore up the coastline. But the loss of mangrove forests ⁴( ) ( ) ( ) ( ) ( ). Climate change is also playing a part.

16

Thanawat Jarupongsakul: The waves and tides and currents are higher than before. Even if you grow a lot of mangroves, it cannot help.

Narrator: The "floating monastery" is now a symbol of Thailand's disappearing shores. But with only six percent of mangroves able to recover and ⁵(   ) (   ) (   ) (   )—many fear it's too little, too late.

---

4 COMPREHENSION CHECK | *Second Viewing*

▷▷ *Watch the news clip again and answer the following questions in English.*

1. At what rate is the seawater advancing every year along some parts of the coastline?

   ....

2. What would people not know if the temple were moved?

   ....

3. How much of the Thai coastline is thought to be affected by coastal erosion?

   ....

4. What are used to shore up the coastline?

   ....

5. What percentage of mangroves can recover?

   ....

5 SUMMARY

 1-08

▷▷ *Listen to the recording and complete the summary.*

As seawaters slowly rose around his temple and his neighbors fled inland, Thai abbot Somnuek Atipanyo ¹(   ) to budge and is today a symbol of the fight to restore the country's fast-eroding coastlines. A dangerous combination of climate change, industrial farming, and rapid ²(   ) is endangering the Gulf of Thailand's coasts, stripping away precious mangrove trees and leaving some buildings like Somnuek's ³(   ) by seawater.

 READING

The United Nations Educational, Scientific and Cultural Organization (UNESCO) lists 1,121 sites worldwide on its heritage list. The oldest of the sites are between 2000 and 5000 years old. Buildings are on the list to protect and preserve them for future generations. For many people, this is a worthwhile and essential goal. However,

5 for others, spending money on old buildings is a wasteful allocation of effort and resources.

There are several reasons why many believe it is vital to preserve these properties. Firstly, because they are part of a town's, city's, or country's identity. The buildings remind each generation of where they have come from, and by sharing a past, they

10 create a sense of community. Secondly, they attract tourists who bring economic benefits to the area. Tourism creates jobs for all the sundry businesses that are part of the industry. Moreover, skilled workers are needed to conserve and restore the buildings. Finally, it promotes civic pride. When people share a community, they tend to work harder on improving living standards.

15 Although they may agree with the idea of conserving buildings, critics claim that the costs are too high. In France, for example, Notre Dame cathedral was badly damaged by fire, and the estimated cost of restoring the building is more than $1 billion. These critics argue that it is better to spend the money on upgrading social infrastructure such as health provision, education, or sports facilities. They say it is

20 more important to think of the people who need help and not old buildings.

Saving historic sites can be expensive, but for many, their value to communities, the money they attract, and the history they represent are worth the cost.

(281 words)

NOTES

allocation 配分   **sundry** 種々の

1 VOCABULARY CHECK

▷▷ *Fill in the blanks with the most appropriate word from the list below.*

1. Egypt is a (   ) country to visit, especially if you are interested in world history.

2. Delegates are going to wear costumes that (   ) the culture of the country.

3. The audience was surprised when the MC revealed the (   ) price of the artwork.

4. One of the goals of the new initiative is to (   ) the biodiversity of the area.

5. The (   ) center holds events for the residents of this community.

estimated   conserve   worthwhile   represent   civic

2 COMPREHENSION QUESTIONS

▷▷ *Answer the following questions in English.*

1. How many sites are listed on UNESCO's heritage list?

   ....

2. What is the first reason why many people believe such sites should be preserved?

   ....

3. What is the second reason?

   ....

4. How much will it cost to restore Notre Dame cathedral?

   ....

5. What examples of social infrastructure does the author provide?

   ....

3 GRAMMAR CHECK

▷▷ *Unscramble the following words and complete the sentences.*

1. This place [town, reminds, me, the, where, of] I grew up.

   This place .... I grew up.

2. [located, largest, the, in, is, third, Japan, lake] in Hokkaido.

   .... in Hokkaido.

3. [temple, tour, visit, to, this, tend, groups] in the evening because it looks particularly beautiful at dusk.

   .... in the evening because it looks particularly beautiful at dusk.

DISCUSSION

Relocating vs Protecting Buildings: How to preserve historical sites

We have heard of many cases of rising sea levels affecting historical buildings.

▷▷ インターネットなどを利用し、文化財保護や浸水対策について調べましょう。保護や対策として堤防などを建設した例、移転した例などについて検討し、下記のどちらの意見を支持するか、主張、理由など自らの考えをまとめ、発表しましょう。

Which opinion do you support and why?

A *Building protection such as dikes and walls are a good solution for allowing historical sites to stay in their original location.*

B *Relocating a historical site is a better solution, and it will be safe for many years.*

自分の意見 _____

理由

_____

_____

_____

_____

REFERENCES

A	**B**
ヴェネツィアを守る（イタリア） ヴェネツィアの街を高潮による浸水の被害から守るため、潟の入り口に可動式の78枚の巨大堤防を建設するという、総額7000億円の国家プロジェクト「モーゼ・プロジェクト」が平成15年（2003）から実施された。 日本の伝統・文化に関する教育推進資料 第34号 2017年10月 https://www.kyoiku.metro.tokyo.lg.jp/school/content/files/documents2017/dentou_suishinsiryo034.pdf	**アブシンベル神殿の移築（エジプト）** 1960年代、ナイル川へのアスワン・ハイ・ダムの建設計画により水没の危機にあったが、ユネスコによって国際的な救済活動が行われた。1964年から1968年の間に、正確に分割されて、約60m上方、ナイル川から210m離れた丘へ、コンクリート製のドームを基盤とする形で移築された。

Disease Prevention vs Economic Growth: Which comes first?

コロナ禍において、観光業や飲食業は大きな打撃を受けています。感染対策として、緊急事態宣言やロックダウンを発令し、人々の動きを止めるべきか、経済活動を優先し、人の動きは制限しない。どちらを優先すべきでしょうか。

I LISTENING

1 KEY WORD STUDY | *Before Watching the Video*

▷▷ *Match each word with its definition.*

1. bleak ( )   2. council ( )   3. destination ( )

4. dire ( )   5. furlough ( )   6. incident ( )

7. overwhelm ( )   8. redress ( )   9. restrict ( )

10. souvenir ( )

a. 悲惨な	b. 一時帰宅させる	c. 調整する	d. 目的地
e. 協議会	f. 圧倒する	g. 制限する	h. お土産
i.（将来などが）暗い	j. 出来事		

2 LISTENING PRACTICE 1 | *First Viewing*   (Time 02:13) 🖥️ WEB動画 💿 DVD

▷▷ *Watch the news clip and write T if the statement is true or F if it is false.*

1. About six million travelers visit Bath in a normal year. ( )

2. The city of Bath relies on British visitors. ( )

3. The Roman Baths are attracting only 30 percent of their usual visitor capacity.

( )

4. Stephen Bird wants to limit the number of people who come in groups. ( )

5. Bournemouth is now encouraging people to visit the town. ( )

WEB動画 DVD CD 1-11

▷▷ *Listen to the recording and fill in the missing words.*

Narrator: In a normal year, the city of Bath welcomes some six million visitors to its hot springs and Georgian terraces, bringing in more than half a billion euros. This year things are much quieter … but despite coronavirus, there are now "some" tourists in town.

Bath パース（英国 Avon 州の都市）

Georgian ジョージ王朝時代風の

Jackie Webb: We're not worried about the pandemic. As long as we ¹( ) ( ) ( ) ( ) ( ) ( ) and everything it's fine.

Cieran Fowley: You're starting to see the sanitization at hotels, the social distancing, so all in all I feel comfortable to travel.

sanitization 衛生化

Narrator: While some British visitors are returning, it's overseas tourists that the city relies on. Souvenir shop owner Marcus Barnes is keeping his store front gleaming … but ²( ) ( ) ( ) ( ), he says the outlook remains bleak.

Marcus Barnes: It's not even a quarter of the business we normally get. I'd say it's like two to three percent. We've had to furlough two staff and get rid of the rest of the staff. We haven't been paid out of this business now for seven months, so things are pretty dire down here.

Narrator: The city's most famous attraction is the Roman Baths, which have seen 2,000 years of change. They've adapted again with new social distancing measures, and they're now welcoming just 30 percent of their usual capacity. But the hope is that this could be an opportunity to re-set ³( ) ( ) ( ) ( ) ( ).

Stephen Bird: We want to restrict the number that come in groups because the larger the number of groups here,

actually, the poorer the quality of visits for everyone else. We think that if we can redress that balance, have fewer people coming but staying longer, putting more into the local economy, actually getting more out of their visit, then that will be ⁴(   ) (   ) (   ) (   ) (   ) (   ) (   ).

Narrator: There's still a clear demand to get away from home. On the hottest day of the year, thousands came to the seaside town of Bournemouth, with the local council declaring a major incident as services were overwhelmed. ⁵(   ) (   ) (   ) (   ) (   ) in Europe could mean more UK residents holidaying at home. The town is now encouraging people to think twice before visiting on busy days. Like Bath and other UK destinations, they'll be trying to strike the right balance between opening the economy and keeping everyone safe.

Bournemouth ボーンマス
（英国南部の都市）

---

4 COMPREHENSION CHECK | *Second Viewing*

▷▷ *Watch the news clip again and answer the following questions in English.*

1. How much money do visitors bring into Bath in a normal year?

   ....

2. Why does Cieran Fowley feel comfortable to travel?

   ....

3. Since the lockdown, what percentage of his usual business is Marcus Barns getting?

   ....

4. What have the Roman Baths seen?

   ....

5. What did Bournemouth council declare on the hottest day of the year?

   ....

▷▷ *Listen to the recording and complete the summary.*

In a normal year the city of Bath welcomes some six million visitors to its hot springs and Georgian terraces, bringing in more than half a billion euros. This year things are much ¹(   ), but despite coronavirus, there are now "some" tourists in town. While some British visitors are returning, it's overseas tourists that the city relies on. The city's most famous ²(   ) is the Roman Baths, which have seen 2,000 years of change. The town is now encouraging people to think twice before visiting on busy days. Like Bath and other UK destinations, the town will be trying to strike the right ³(   ) between opening the economy and keeping everyone safe.

▌ READING

 1-13

In the past 100 years, there have been three global pandemics. Following each, health experts were better able
5 to understand how viruses spread and how officials should respond. Covid-19 has, to date, resulted in approximately 3.2 million deaths and locked down
10 economies worldwide. The loss of life is tragic, but many fear a locked-down country with a stalled economy will create even more hardship.

Those wanting an open economy believe a situation where people cannot
15 make a living is a more serious threat than a virus. The demands of self-isolation and workplace closures remove the means to earn a wage. In these circumstances, many people are unable to prevent themselves from falling into poverty. Without work, families become more vulnerable and face even more significant health risks. A lockdown means producers of goods cannot supply markets, and closed borders
20 reduce trade flow. The result is that governments receive less tax to support those most at risk from closures and job loss.

On the other hand, many believe that it is right to put the protection of life first.

Limiting human contact stops high levels of transmission. Social distancing prevents the deaths of those with underlying health problems who are most vulnerable to the virus. Statistics, however, show that as the virus mutates, there is, to some degree, a more potent threat to all age groups. A return to pre-covid conditions risks higher numbers of sick patients and more pressure on medical services.

Virus waves will more likely continue until everyone has received a vaccine. The challenge is to balance safety and the needs for the economy to prevent further infections.

(270 words)

NOTES

stalled 行き詰まった　**mutate** 変異する

1 VOCABULARY CHECK

▷▷ *Fill in the blanks with the most appropriate word from the list below.*

1. Researchers (　　　　) that the increase of human activity in the area will have a negative impact on the local ecosystem.

2. The company has agreed to (　　　　) medicine to the newly established hospital.

3. This vaccine is (　　　　) to heat and has to be stored in a specialized freezer.

4. Universities have played a (　　　　) role in developing a system of online education.

5. One of the emerging problems of today's society is social (　　　　) experienced by younger generations.

supply　fear　potent　isolation　vulnerable

2 COMPREHENSION QUESTIONS

▷ *Answer the following questions in English.*

1. What have health experts understood through global pandemics?

   ....

2. What do those who want an open economy believe?

   ....

3. What do closed borders reduce?

   ....

4. How can we stop high levels of transmission?

   ....

5. What might a return to pre-Covid conditions lead to?

   ....

3 GRAMMAR CHECK

▷ *Unscramble the following words and complete the sentences.*

1. The university lounge is [students, socialize, can, with, where, friends, their] in a relaxed atmosphere.

   The university lounge is ....in a relaxed atmosphere.

2. The number of pet owners [continue, increase, because, will, to, likely] pets can provide healing.

   The number of pet owners .... pets can provide healing.

3. Different genres of music [several, popular, past, become, years, the, have, in] in Japan.

   Different genres of music .... in Japan.

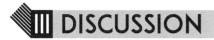 DISCUSSION

Disease Prevention vs Economic Growth: Which comes first?

The impacts of the pandemic and the economic fallout have been widespread.

▷▷ インターネットなどを利用し、コロナウイルス感染症予防対策と経済発展について調べましょう。コロナウイルス感染症予防対策、経済発展への影響、予防接種の拡大による新たな生活様式の可能性などについても検討し、下記のどちらの意見を支持するか、主張、理由など自らの考えをまとめ、発表しましょう。

Which opinion do you support and why?

A *We need to protect people from contracting diseases first and economic growth will come after.*

B *We should put our top priority on economic growth without worrying about disease prevention.*

自分の意見 _____

理由

_____
_____
_____
_____

REFERENCES

新型コロナウイルス感染症と両立する経済活動の再加速に向けて

新型コロナウイルス感染症の流行の端緒から今日に至るまでの数か月の間に、わが国の社会全体に大きな変化が生じている。緊急事態宣言という、誰しも予想しなかった状況下で、課題と同時に、日本の可能性も明らかとなった。今後のウィズコロナ時代においては、個々人が新しい生活様式を実践するのみならず、今回得られた経験をもとに、新しい社会づくりに挑戦していかなければならない。

一般社団法人日本経済団体連合会　新型コロナウイルス会議 2020 年 7 月 https://www.keidanren.or.jp/policy/2020/065_honbun.pdf

Extracurricular Activity vs Studying Hard: Discipline for preventing crimes

犯罪防止のために課外活動は有益でしょうか。学校での学習活動のほかに、犯罪防止として役立つのはどのような活動でしょうか。学習に集中するだけが良いか、課外活動にも取り組むべきか、考えましょう。

I LISTENING

1 KEY WORD STUDY | *Before Watching the Video*

▷▷ *Match each word with its definition.*

1. accessible   (   )   2. affirmation   (   )   3. conductor   (   )

4. inequality   (   )   5. negligence   (   )   6. participate   (   )

7. prestigious   (   )   8. refuge   (   )   9. reputation   (   )

10. riot   (   )

a. 指揮者	b. 肯定	c. 権威のある	d. 参加する
e. 接近できる	f. 過失	g. 評判	h. 暴動
i. 不平等	j. 避難所		

2 LISTENING PRACTICE 1 | *First Viewing*   (Time 02:20) 📺 💿 DVD

▷▷ *Watch the news clip and write T if the statement is true or F if it is false.*

1. OrchKids is a program aiming to inspire social change through music education.

(   )

2. Homicide and violent crime rates in Baltimore are among the lowest in the US.

(   )

3. Stefany dreams of becoming a conductor of OrchKids one day.   (   )

4. Marin Alsop became the first female conductor of a major US orchestra.   (   )

5. When Freddie Gray was killed by police negligence, Baltimore's reputation for violence and inequality became well known worldwide.   (   )

3 LISTENING PRACTICE 2

WEB動画 💻 DVD 🎬 CD 💿 1-15

▷▷ *Listen to the recording and fill in the missing words.*

Narrator: In this West Baltimore school ... this cacophony of notes marks the sound of a 60-student orchestra. These young musicians are part of OrchKids, a program that aims to inspire social change through musical education. [1]( ) ( ) ( ) ( )( ) ( ) ( ), more than 1,000 elementary school students now find refuge here from the streets of Baltimore—whose homicide and violent crime rates are among the highest in the US.

cacophony 不快な音調

OrchKids The Baltimore Symphony Orchestra の子供向け課外活動事業

homicide 殺人

Jane Cromwell: Many of those kids take two or three buses from another part of town after school to travel to where we meet. [2]( ) ( ) ( ) ( ) ( ) ( ). It means that they have to leave or sacrifice doing other things in their schools and they do it.

Narrator: Stefany has been practicing the cello here four times a week for the past seven years. She says [3]( ) ( ) ( ) ( ) ( ) ( ) before joining the program. Now, Stefany dreams of one day teaching it, and has even been chosen to participate in a prestigious summer program in Michigan.

Stefany: Some of them they didn't like it at the moment but then I tell them it's something very nice, it's something that gets you away from bad influences, and it can really have a positive change in your life.

Narrator: OrchKids is the brainchild of Marin Alsop, who became the first female conductor of a major US orchestra when she joined the Baltimore Symphony in 2007. Alsop [4]( ) ( ) ( ) ( ) ( ) to make classical

brainchild 新構想
Marin Alsop アメリカ人指揮者、バイオリニスト(1956 ～)

29

music more accessible to Baltimore's youth.

Marín Alsop: Through programs like OrchKids they start to see a different kind of future. You know they're able to travel, to play, they're ^5(   ) (   ) (   ) (   ) (   ) (   ) (   ) (   ), they're on stage, they're receiving positive affirmation for what they're doing.

Narrator: Baltimore's reputation for violence and social inequality crossed international radars when the city erupted in riots in 2015 over the death of Freddie Gray, a black man killed due to police negligence. OrchKids is looking to change their reputation by turning Baltimore into a city of music rather than crime.

Freddie Gray 2015年4月に警察に逮捕された際に死亡したアフリカ系アメリカ人

---

4 | COMPREHENSION CHECK | *Second Viewing*

WEB動画　DVD

▷▷ *Watch the news clip again and answer the following questions in English.*

1. What creates the loud sound of musical notes in a west Baltimore school?

   ....

2. How often has Stefany been practicing the cello?

   ....

3. What does Stefany tell other kids about OrchKids?

   ....

4. What do children start to see through programs like OrchKids?

   ....

5. Why did Baltimore erupt in riots in 2015?

   ....

5 | SUMMARY

CD 1-16

▷▷ *Listen to the recording and complete the summary.*

In this West Baltimore school, this cacophony of notes marks the sound of a 60-student orchestra. More than 1,000 elementary school students now find ^1(   ) here from the streets of Baltimore whose homicide and violent crime rates are among the highest in the US. OrchKids is the brainchild of Marin Alsop. The city's reputation for violence and social ²(   ) crossed international radars when the city erupted in riots in 2015 over the death of Freddie Gray, a Black man killed due to police negligence. OrchKids is looking to change this reputation by ³(   ) Baltimore as a city of music rather than crime.

 READING

While in school or college, many students take part in outside activities. For some, it is a chance to use their talents, learn new skills, and make friends. For a few, it allows them to manage their time and energy. This keeps them from anti-social behavior. For others, however, the activities distract from academic studies.

5   Many people believe that extracurricular activities are a general benefit to students. They say that activities can reinforce students' classroom knowledge. Some studies indicate a link between taking part in outside activities and how well students do in exams. Activities that involve problem-solving, creativity, or critical thinking can often assist with academic subjects. Furthermore, activities teach discipline.

10   For example, they prepare students to persevere with complex tasks, and they train them in time management. In addition, activities can teach students to become more confident when they meet new people.

However, some disagree with how much time students should put into extracurricular activities. They argue that spending too much time on activities

15   outside the classroom can reduce, not increase, grades. They claim that many students have their life planned from a young age. In this case, they cannot cope with unstructured time at college. The classroom, they say, provides the right conditions for support. They argue that study is the best way to teach self-discipline. It guides learning and models good behavior. They say that the basic manners, emphasis on

20   rules, and feedback in the classroom are of more value than activities.

The evidence suggests that classrooms do provide the setting for students to succeed. However, it shows there are also lessons to be learned from other activities.

(272 words)

NOTES

extracurricular 課外の   **persevere** やり抜く

1 | VOCABULARY CHECK

▷ Fill in the blanks with the most appropriate word from the list below.

1. Using your smartphone while walking may (   ) your attention.

2. The problem looked simple enough, but it turned out to be quite (   ).

3. Repetition is the key to (   ) our memory.

4. Attending a good school does not automatically guarantee (   ) success.

5. Jeff was able to (   ) with the challenge by analyzing the situation carefully.

> reinforce   distract   cope   complex   academic

2 | COMPREHENSION QUESTIONS

▷ Answer the following questions in English.

1. What connection do some studies show between outside activities and exams?

    ....

2. What kind of activities can assist with academic subjects?

    ....

3. What can extracurricular activities teach students to become?

    ....

4. Why do some people think students cannot cope with unstructured time at college?

    ....

5. Why do some people argue that study is the best way to teach self-discipline?

    ....

3 | GRAMMAR CHECK

▷ Unscramble the following words and complete the sentences.

1. Mia [spending, her, with, friends, time, enjoys] at a café after classes.

    Mia .... at a café after classes.

2. Riding a bicycle uphill [walking, tiring, tends, than, more, be, to].

    Riding a bicycle uphill ....

3. The NGO calculated [a, to, it, much, build, school, cost, how, would] in the town.

    The NGO calculated .... in the town.

DISCUSSION

Extracurricular Activity vs Studying Hard:
Discipline for preventing crimes

Some studies have shown being involved in extracurricular activities reduces the likelihood of dropping out of school and committing a criminal offense and leads to higher educational retainment and success and achievements in school work.

▷▷ インターネットなどを利用し、課外活動と犯罪防止について調べましょう。課外活動や犯罪防止など良い点ばかりでなく、学習活動への影響など悪い点についても検討し、下記のどちらの意見を支持するか、主張、理由など自らの考えをまとめ、発表しましょう。

Which opinion do you support and why?

A *Extracurricular activities are important for preventing crimes.*

B *Studying hard develops discipline, and there is no need for extra activities.*

自分の意見 _____

理由

_____

_____

_____

_____

REFERENCES

『中学・高校の部活動が生徒の自己形成に及ぼす影響』小川潔・岡田大爾 広島国際大学教職教室　教育論叢 (9), 11-21, 2017-12-20
特別活動の趣旨に関連した中学・高校における部活動は、大学生の人格の完成に結びつく自己形成にどう影響したのか、大学の授業で振り返る演習を行い、部活動の意義及び課題を分析する中で明らかにした。

Traditional Living vs Urbanization: Is noise pollution?

都会での生活を逃れ、田舎暮らしを始める人が増えています。家畜の鳴き声や自然の音は騒音でしょうか。田舎の日常風景の一部として受け入れるべきでしょうか。都市化、田舎の生活など、騒音について議論しましょう。

I LISTENING

1 KEY WORD STUDY | *Before Watching the Video*

▷▷ *Match each word with its definition.*

1. accuse ( )   2. bother ( )   3. constituent ( )

4. dispute ( )   5. disgrace ( )   6. heritage ( )

7. impose ( )   8. pending ( )   9. rowdy ( )

10. rural ( )

> a. 不名誉   b. 悩ます   c. 騒々しい   d. 係争中の
>
> e. 選挙区民   f. 論争   g. 押しつける   h. いなかの
>
> i. 非難する   j. 遺産

2 LISTENING PRACTICE 1 | *First Viewing*   (Time 02:46) WEB動画 🖥 🄳 DVD

▷▷ *Watch the news clip and write T if the statement is true or F if it is false.*

1. The mayor of Gajac believes the sounds of the countryside should be granted heritage protection. ( )

2. A woman was taken to court because her rooster broke into a neighbor's house.

   ( )

3. In Gajac, the bells are silent and there have been no arguments. ( )

4. The mayor wants people to stop bringing lawsuits against noises in the future.

   ( )

5. A mayor in southeast of France received complaints that cicadas were noisy. ( )

3 | LISTENING PRACTICE 2

 WEB動画 DVD CD 1-19

▷▷ *Listen to the recording and fill in the missing words.*

Narrator: Are these quintessentially French symbols under threat? That's what the mayor of Gajac, a small village in the south-west of France, believes. He says the sounds of the countryside should be granted heritage protection ... ¹(　　　) (　　　) (　　　) (　　　) (　　　), bothered by the noise, are suing villagers.

Bruno Dionis du Séjour: It's a disgrace that rural people have to go to court because of people who come from elsewhere. People from the city are welcome in the countryside but  only if they respect it, as it is, that's all. We're not asking any more than that! ²(　　　) (　　　) (　　　) (　　　) (　　　), do I ask for the traffic lights and cars to be removed?

Narrator: In one high-profile case, a woman is being taken to court by the owners of a second home on Oléron island, off the French Atlantic coast. They accuse her rooster of being too rowdy.

Bruno Dionis du Séjour: The rooster is after all the symbol of France. While we glorify the cockerel of Notre Dame cathedral, we should at least let our roosters crow if they want to! ³(　　　) (　　　) (　　　) (　　　) (　　　) (　　　), just for people to be reasonable, that's all.

Narrator: Silencing the bells is out of the question in Gajac, and there are no cases pending. But this local man says there have been disputes.

Jean-Claude Houques: People complained about the noise that the rooster made, and then at noon, that the bells rang. At some point they had to decide if what they wanted was to be in the country and hear the bells and

quintessentially 典型的に

Gajac（フランス南西部の村）

Oléron island /oʊˈlɪrən/ フランス南部大西洋上の島

cockerel 若いおんどり（雄のニワトリ）

Notre Dame cathedral ノートルダム寺院［大聖堂］（パリの中心部シテ島にあるカトリック教会）

35

live a peaceful, quiet life. In the end ⁴(   )
(   ) (   ) (   ).

Narrator: The mayor wrote to his constituents about his frustration. Since then, he has received ⁵(   ) (   ) (   ) (   ) (   ) daily, from all over France. The number of noise complaints has gone up and up in recent years: in 2016, a couple in southwestern France were forced to fill in a pond, after their frogs were accused of croaking too loudly. Last summer, a mayor in the southeast of the country received complaints from holidaymakers who wanted to silence the cicadas. Now Gajac's mayor is hoping that MPs will act quickly to stop urbanites imposing their ways on rural French life.

cicada セミ

MPs 下院議員

4 COMPREHENSION CHECK | *Second Viewing*

WEB動画 DVD

▷▷ *Watch the news clip again and answer the following questions in English.*

1. Why have rural people been taken to court?

   ....

2. What is the symbol of France?

   ....

3. What do newcomers in Gajac complain about?

   ....

4. Why has the mayor written to his constituents?

   ....

5. What did a couple in southwestern France have to do in 2016?

   ....

5 SUMMARY

 1-20

▷▷ *Listen to the recording and complete the summary.*

A French court is set to rule this week on whether an early-rising cockerel should be considered a neighborly nuisance in a case that has led to crows of protest in the countryside. A woman from the ¹( ) island of Oléron off France's western coast has been summoned to court on Thursday after a legal complaint by her neighbors who are ²( ) by the early crowing of her rooster during their holidays. The case has attracted attention because the rooster is an emblem of France, while the plaintiffs have been ³( ) as pushy urbanites who keep their property in Saint-Pierre-d'Oléron as a second home.

▌ READING

 1-21

Each year, the populations of cities and towns across the world expand. Those living in more rural communities are increasingly moving to urban centers, searching for work and opportunities. However, the noise from these growing areas harms both the residents and the biodiversity from the surrounding regions.

5 Studies show sound itself is not a problem. The countryside can be a noisy place. Farming and other land use, for example, raise the levels of noise. Many species use sound when looking for a mate or warning of danger. Moreover, natural events, such as weather conditions, create noise. The problems occur when noise from people, traffic, or industry becomes constant.

10 Several studies show that, for humans, exposure to high levels of noise can lead to higher risks of heart problems or stroke. The noise activates a person's response system and puts pressure on body processes. For animals, there seem to be two main problems that occur. The first is that noise hides common animal sounds. With other harmful effects such as light pollution or aircraft noise, there is a substantial
15 influence on wildlife communication, location, or reproduction. The second problem is the stress that noise pollution can produce. As animals rely first and foremost on audio cues when hunting or for safety, continual noise results in a constant state of alert and increases stress.

It is fair to say that most people appreciate the sounds of the countryside. That
20 is to say; they enjoy sounds that are mostly quieter than those found in urban areas. But the constant growth of cities steadily decreases surrounding wildlife habitats and now threatens the people and the species that live there.

(275 words)

NOTES

biodiversity 生物多様性　　**first and foremost** 何よりもまず

1 | VOCABULARY CHECK

▷▷ *Fill in the blanks with the most appropriate word from the list below.*

1. We are waiting for the (   ) to start the surprise birthday party.

2. A (   ) amount of precious metals was discovered in the seabed.

3. Too much (   ) to the sunlight is harmful for the skin.

4. Wild animals have to always stay (   ) to predators.

5. The month of June in Japan is characterized by (   ) rain.

> cue substantial continual exposure alert

2 | COMPREHENSION QUESTIONS

▷▷ *Answer the following questions in English.*

1. Why do people move from rural communities to urban centers?

   ....

2. When do animals use sound?

   ....

3. What can lead to higher risks of heart problems or stroke?

   ....

4. What kind of influence does noise have on wildlife?

   ....

5. Why does noise pollution cause stress in animals?

   ....

3 | GRAMMAR CHECK

▷▷ *Unscramble the following words and complete the sentences.*

1. According to research, [region, snowfall, this, unusual, have, to, for, is, it] in October.

   According to research, ...in October.

2. Miscalculation of the initial data [in, of, the, the, resulted, failure, study].

   Miscalculation of the initial data ....

3. Sleep deprivation may [level, concentration, of, decreased, to, a, lead].

   Sleep deprivation may ....

38

 # DISCUSSION

Traditional Living vs Urbanization: Is noise pollution?

There are many discussions about the definition of noise pollution.
Which opinion do you support and why?

▷▷ カエルの鳴き声、蝉の声などは、騒音でしょうか。インターネットなどを利用し、自然の音と騒音公害の問題について調べましょう。都会と田舎の暮らしの違いなども視野に、下記のどちらの意見を支持するか、主張、理由などの考えをまとめ、発表しましょう。

Which opinion do you support and why?

A *I prefer traditional living, and love the sound of nature.*

B *I prefer an urban life, and I consider animal sounds to be noise pollution.*

自分の意見

理由

_____
_____
_____
_____

REFERENCES	
A	**B**
隣の庭のカエルの鳴き声は騒音か？ 「自然音」と訴え退ける判決 「隣の庭のカエルがうるさい」として住民が騒音の差し止めやカエルの駆除を求めた訴えについて、東京地方裁判所は「カエルの鳴き声は自然音で騒音には当たらない」として退ける判決を言い渡した。 NHK 2021年4月 https://www3.nhk.or.jp/news/html/20210423/k10012993871000.html	騒音に係る環境基準について 環境基本法第16条第1項の規定に基づく、騒音に係る環境上の条件について生活環境を保全し、人の健康の保護に資する上で維持されることが望ましい基準 環境省 2012年3月 http://www.env.go.jp/kijun/oto1-1.html

Fair Trade vs Free Trade: What is best for farmers?

発展等途上国の農家を保護するためにフェアトレードの考えが生まれました。一方では、自由な貿易、経済の利点を主張する人々もいます。発展途上国の農家、先進国の消費者にとって良いのはどちらでしょうか。

I LISTENING

1 | KEY WORD STUDY | *Before Watching the Video*

▷▷ *Match each word with its definition.*

1. account for ( ) 2. compensation ( ) 3. in conjunction with ( )

4. decent ( ) 5. encouraging ( ) 6. envisage ( )

7. fertilizer ( ) 8. implement ( ) 9. lush ( )

10. potentially ( )

a. 期待する	b. 適正な	c. 講じる	d. 肥料
e. 励みになる	f. 潜在的に	g. 〜と共に	h. 報酬
i. 占める	j. 豊かな		

2 | LISTENING PRACTICE 1 | *First Viewing*　(Time 02:18) WEB動画 DVD

▷▷ *Watch the news clip and write T if the statement is true or F if it is false.*

1. Cocoa is one of the most important crops in Ghana's exports. ( )

2. The price of cocoa per ton is to be established in conjunction with the Ivory Coast at 2,600 USD. ( )

3. There have traditionally been 50 big chocolate-producing companies in Ghana. ( )

4. Ruth Amoah sells an artisanal chocolate product called Moments. ( )

5. Ghana and the Ivory Coast produce 60 percent of the world's cocoa. ( )

3 LISTENING PRACTICE 2

WEB動画 DVD CD 1-23

▷▷ *Listen to the recording and fill in the missing words.*

Narrator: In the lush green forests of Mampong in Central Ghana, cocoa trees are one of the most common sights. Cocoa is one of the most important crops in Ghana's exports. Many of those involved in cocoa production were delighted by a recent government announcement that ¹( ) ( ) ( ) ( ) ( ) ( ) for the product on the international market. They envisage a positive impact across the supply chain that would bring benefit to each individual cocoa farmer.

Mampong（ガーナの都市）

Kwame: So, if the government is going to increase the price, it means he can afford a fertilizer, he can afford the weedicide, ²( ) ( ) ( ) ( ) ( ), so he can increase his production. So, when his production also increases, it means he's going to get more money because prices are going to go up.

he → the farmer

weedicide 除草剤

Narrator: The price is to be set at 2,600 USD per ton of cocoa, an amount established in conjunction with the Ivory Coast. The idea is to guarantee what is being termed as a decent compensation for producers. Recently, the price of cocoa on the global market has been as low as 1,961 USD per ton, making this increase a major step. Members of the Ghanaian Farmers Association ³( ) ( ) ( ) ( ) ( ) this government intervention.

Ivory Coast アイボリーコースト（コートジボワールの別称）

Ghanaian Farmers Association ガーナ農民協会

Alhaji Alhassan Bukari: We don't have anything to sell unless the cocoa. So, if the government are thinking about the farmers, and they come together to fight for the farmers, we support them.

41

Narrator: But it's not just the cocoa farmers who stand to gain from this new set price, as chocolatiers will also feel the impact. In Ghana there have traditionally been only two

big chocolate-producing companies, but around 50 smaller businesses have emerged in recent years. Four years ago, Ruth Amoah founded her chocolate brand called Moments, marketed as an artisanal product, with the line "From bean to bar." 4(   ) (   ) (   ) (   ).

Ruth Amoah: People will probably decide they would want to even kind of produce their products from here. Because it may be cheaper to even make your chocolate in Ghana and

ship it out. So, potentially, that could be more work, more white-label chocolate that we can be doing for other companies. So, I think it's also encouraging for people who are in the industry.

white-label 白いラベルの（品名・製造社名などを明記していない）

Narrator: The governments of Ghana and the Ivory Coast are now set to discuss how best to implement this measure 5(   ) (   ) (   ) (   ) (   ) of cocoa production.

With these two countries together accounting for 60 percent of the world's cocoa production, there will surely be a major knock-on effect on chocolate producers the world over.

knock-on effect ドミノ効果、連鎖反応

4 COMPREHENSION CHECK | *Second Viewing*

▷▷ *Watch the news clip again and answer the following questions in English.*

1. How did people involved in cocoa production feel about a recent government announcement of a set minimum price of cocoa?

   ....

2. What do the cocoa farmers expect when their production increases?

   ....

3. What has the cocoa price been recently on the global market?

   ....

4. What will the farmers do if the government fights for them?

   ....

5. Why are people in Ghana deciding to produce their products in Ghana?

   ....

5 SUMMARY

 1-24

▷▷ *Listen to the recording and complete the summary.*

Cocoa is one of the most important crops in Ghana's exports. Many of those involved in cocoa production were [1](   ) by a recent government announcement that a minimum price would be set for the product on the international market. The governments of Ghana and the Ivory Coast are now set to discuss how best to [2](   ) this measure for the next two years of cocoa production. With these two countries together accounting for 60 percent of the world's cocoa production, there will surely be a major knock-on effect on chocolate [3](   ) the world over.

Ⅱ READING

 1-25

Globalization is a system that enables a free flow of goods and services between countries. Those who favor the system claim that fewer border limits benefit buyers, sellers, and markets across the world. In contrast, campaigners for an equal system oppose the claim. They argue that fewer limits also mean greater exploitation. They
5   say free trade allows unjust practices to occur in mainly developing countries. These practices are often damaging to an economy and to the people it supports. They argue that there should be more protection for workers' conditions, rights, and pay.

Those who argue for free trade say that the system can lower costs and increase standards. It is cheaper because low-cost countries make the products. First, firms produce goods in countries with the cheapest resources. Then, the goods are returned to home markets and sold for higher prices. Using natural resources specific to that country provides local people with jobs. Moreover, it introduces new technology and partnerships. Free trade, they claim, expands the marketplace and promotes higher living standards.

However, others argue that free trade is one-sided. They support fair trade as it gives people in poorer nations a better chance to benefit from their labor. Larger numbers of farmers or factory workers in less developed countries can better support themselves and their families. If parents can support their families, it will likely result in fewer child workers, better social conditions, and improved community services. Fair trade, they say, brings balance between economies.

Free trade does seem to benefit some countries over others. If all nations are to experience gains from globalization, it is crucial to establish a system that genuinely allows everyone to benefit.   (278 words)

NOTES

free trade 自由貿易   **fair trade** フェア・トレード、公平な貿易

1 VOCABULARY CHECK

▷▷ *Fill in the blanks with the most appropriate word from the list below.*

1. It is (   ) that we face the problem of the unequal distribution of wealth.

2. The campaign tried to raise awareness against (   ) of forest resources.

3. The company appealed to the court to dispute the (   ) allegation filed by its competitor.

4. I am (   ) excited to visit Africa for the first time in my life.

5. Sophia said she would help me with the project on the (   ) that I treat her to lunch.

unjust   crucial genuinely condition exploitation

2 COMPREHENSION QUESTIONS

▷▷ *Answer the following questions in English.*

1. What do those who favor globalization claim?

   ....

2. Where do firms produce goods in order to lower costs?

   ....

3. What is an advantage of using natural resources specific to the country?

   ....

4. What is a benefit of fair trade to those in poorer nations?

   ....

5. What impact will there be on society when people can support their families better?

   ....

3 GRAMMAR CHECK

▷▷ *Unscramble the following words and complete the sentences.*

1. Apples harvested in Japan tend to be large and round [in, in, those, contrast, America, grown, to].

   Apples harvested in Japan tend to be large and round ....

   ....

2. [hours, there, time, between, of, nine, difference, are] Japan and Ghana.

   .... Japan and Ghana.

3. You should bring a cardigan [cold, case, gets, in, it, you, with] at night.

   You should bring a cardigan ....at night.

 # DISCUSSION

Fair Trade vs Free Trade: What is best for farmers?

What are the benefits and the disadvantages of fair trade and free trade?

▷ インターネットなどを利用し、フェアトレードについて調べましょう。フェアトレードの発展や今後の可能性など良い点ばかりでなく、自由経済や地域社会への影響など悪い点についても検討し、下記のどちらの意見を支持するか、主張、理由など自らの考えをまとめ、発表しましょう。

Which opinion do you support and why?

> **A** *Fair trade is the best way to protect local farmers in developing countries.*

> **B** *Free trade is the best way for the economy to flourish.*

自分の意見

理由

REFERENCES	
A	**B**
フェアトレード (公正な貿易) 貧困のない公正な社会をつくるために、途上国の経済的社会的に弱い立場にある生産者と経済的社会的に強い立場にある先進国の消費者が対等な立場で行う貿易。適正な賃金の支払いや労働環境の整備などを通して生産者の生活向上を図ることが第一の目的。 特定非営利活動法人シャプラニール https://www.shaplaneer.org/fairtrade/about/	**自由貿易** 輸出入について、国が介入や干渉しない貿易。自由貿易は国内企業だけでなく外国企業との自由競争を促し、製造者や生産者は、ライバルに負けないようにより良い商品を作る。消費者は、同じものを買うときに商品の選択肢が増え、安く買えるようになる。 みんなの仕事 Lab 2018 年 5 月 https://lab.pasona.co.jp/trade/word/503/

Environmental Activism vs International Agreements: Which is better?

地球温暖化対策としてパリ議定書、環境保護のためにラムサール条約などが締結されています。一方では、いろいろな活動家が人々に訴える活動に取り組んでいます。環境保護に活躍しているのはどちらだと思いますか。

I LISTENING

1 KEY WORD STUDY | *Before Watching the Video*

▷▷ *Match each word with its definition.*

1. ban   (   )   2. canal   (   )   3. climate   (   )

4. conference   (   )   5. convince   (   )   6. enforce   (   )

7. inspire   (   )   8. ministry   (   )   9. polluter   (   )

10. suffocating   (   )

a. 省	b. 息苦しい	c. 汚染者	d. 禁止する
e. 実施する	f. 気候	g. 会議	h. 説得する
i. 運河	j. 触発させる		

2 LISTENING PRACTICE 1 | *First Viewing*   (Time 01:38) 🖥 DVD

▷▷ *Watch the news clip and write T if the statement is true or F if it is false.*

1. The area in Bangkok has solved the problem of plastic garbage.   (   )

2. Lilly thinks kids can make a difference.   (   )

3. Thailand is the world's biggest polluter of the ocean.   (   )

4. Lilly and her fellow activists clean up the city's parks.   (   )

5. Lilly's goal is to ban single-use plastic bags by 2022.   (   )

WEB動画 DVD CD 1-27

▷▷ *Listen to the recording and fill in the missing words.*

Narrator: This area of Bangkok is known as the city's green lung. But it's suffocating under plastic like much of the country. Lilly is just 12, yet ¹( ) ( ) ( ) ( ) to clean up the city, inspired by young Swedish climate change superstar Greta Thunberg.

Greta Thunberg スウェーデンの環境活動家

Ralyn Satidtanasarn "Lilly": Greta is really important to me 'cause for what she symbolizes. She says that kids can make a difference. She wants everybody to do something and ²( ) ( ) ( ) ( ) ( ) ( ).

Narrator: Thailand is the world's sixth biggest polluter of the oceans. Every Thai person uses on average eight plastic bags a day. Lilly is taking her message to the top. She has led several sit-ins outside the government house, ³( ) ( ) ( ) ( ), and she spoke at this UN conference.

sit-in 座り込み（抗議・デモ）

Ralyn Satidtanasarn "Lilly": I'm trying to enforce a lesson onto the Ministry of Education, a lesson about the environment.

Narrator: She and fellow activists also clean up the city's canals.

Ralyn Satidtanasarn "Lilly": It is hard, but I would like to be positive about it because there's always hope we can always fix something. If there's a problem, ⁴( ) ( ) ( ).

Narrator: Lilly's goal is to ban single-use plastic bags by 2022. ⁵( ) ( ) ( ), managing to convince a supermarket chain in Bangkok not to offer plastic bags one day a week.

4 COMPREHENSION CHECK | *Second Viewing*

▷▷ *Watch the news clip again and answer the following questions in English.*

1. Who has inspired Lilly to fight to clean up the city?

    ....

2. Why is Greta Thunberg important to Lilly?

    ....

3. On average, how many plastic bags does a Thai person use every day?

    ....

4. What lesson does Lilly try to enforce to the Ministry of Education?

    ....

5. What was Lilly's first victory?

    ....

5 SUMMARY

1-28

▷▷ *Listen to the recording and complete the summary.*

The area known as Bangkok's green lung is suffocating under plastic like much of the country. Lilly is just 12, but she is leading the ¹(   ) to clean up the city, inspired by young Swedish climate change superstar Greta Thunberg. Lilly's goal is to ²(   ) single-use plastic bags by 2022. Her first victory was managing to convince a supermarket chain in Bangkok not to offer ³(   ) bags one day a week.

II READING

1-29

   Plastic and other debris increasingly litter the world's oceans. The amount of waste in the water is resulting in significant damage to marine species. One of the most pressing problems facing societies is deciding who is responsible for cleaning the oceans of microplastic, nets, and other pollution. Some say it is governments, ⁵ some say businesses, while others argue it is the responsibility of each person.

   While it may be true that a government manages trash collection, large amounts of waste are beyond national lines. No government is liable for the areas outside its borders. The outcome is that no government is accountable for cleaning the oceans.

Nevertheless, many say that only
10 states have the resources to carry
out large projects. Moreover, they
also have the assets to manage waste
before it enters the oceans. Many
claim that leaders are not robust
15 enough in regulating the sources of
pollution or tough enough on those
who break the rules.

On the other hand, some say that companies should pay for clean-up. They say
that businesses create large amounts of waste in the air, land, and waterways. They
20 should therefore pay higher environmental taxes to offset the damage caused by their
products. Many believe that companies are not held accountable for the large amount
of waste they dump in the oceans.

A third group blamed for the levels of debris is individual people. Critics say they
should be more responsible for discarded containers and wrapping. Some say there
25 should be more education about recycling. If respecting the environment is taught
to young people, things will gradually change. With so much debris clogging the
world's oceans, it is clear that someone must take action before a dangerous situation
becomes unmanageable.

(286 words)

NOTES

debris がらくた、ゴミ **litter** 散らかす **accountable** 責任がある **offset** 相殺する

1 VOCABULARY CHECK

▷▷ *Fill in the blanks with the most appropriate word from the list below.*

1. Cans and plastic bottles are examples of recyclable (   ).

2. It is necessary to take (   ) actions against environmental risks.

3. Patrick's group decided to (   ) the plan after thorough consideration.

4. Your kitchen drain can (   ) if you do not regularly clean it.

5. Diana has decided to (   ) the challenges in her life rather than
   avoiding them.

> discard   face   robust   trash   clog

2 COMPREHENSION QUESTIONS

▷▷ *Answer the following questions in English.*

1. What major problem is the amount of waste in the water causing?

   ....

2. What is the outcome of governments not being liable for the areas outside their borders?

   ....

3. What does the author imply that leaders should do?

   ....

4. Why do some people think companies should pay higher environmental taxes?

   ....

5. What do critics say individuals should be more responsible for?

   ....

3 GRAMMAR CHECK

▷▷ *Unscramble the following words and complete the sentences.*

1. Oscar [his, blamed, away, for, brother, throwing] his clothes.
   Oscar .... his clothes.

2. Please show your ID card to the security guard [headquarters, you, company, before, the, enter].
   Please show your ID card to the security guard ....
   ....

3. Japan has been [leading, develop, countries, one, the, to, of] environmentally friendly products.
   Japan has been ....environmentally friendly products.

III DISCUSSION

Environmental Activism vs International Agreements
Which is better?

Which do you think plays a more important role in preserving the environment?

▷▷ インターネットなどを利用し、気候サミット・環境活動家について調べましょう。京都議定書やパリ協定などの国際的な地球温暖化対策や気候変動に対する枠組み条約、グレタ・トゥンベリさんに代表されるような環境活動家について調べ、下記のどちらの意見を支持するか、主張、理由など自らの考えをまとめ、発表しましょう。

Which opinion do you support and why?

A *Environmental activists should play a more important role in preserving the environment, and so we need to educate young people about ecology.*

B *International agreements such as the Kyoto Protocol and the Paris Protocol of 2015 have an important role in preserving the environment, and so we should rely on political leaders.*

自分の意見 ＿＿＿＿＿＿＿＿

理由

＿＿

＿＿

＿＿

REFERENCES

気候サミット
2021 年 4 月 22 から 23 日、米国主催により気候サミット「Leaders Summit on Climate」がオンライン形式で開催された。

「目をそらすな」 グレタさん、米議会で証言 (2021 年 04 月 23 日)
スウェーデンの環境活動家グレタ・トゥンベリさん（１８）が２２日、米下院監視・改革委員会の環境小委員会で「いつまで気候変動から目をそらし続けられると考えているのか」と証言し、本腰を入れて対策に乗り出すよう要請した。とりわけ温室効果ガス排出産業に対する優遇措置の継続を「恥だ」と糾弾した。（ワシントン時事 2021 年 4 月）

Alternative vs Fossil Energy: Power for the Future

自然エネルギーの導入や効率の向上をめざし、グリーン水素の開発が進められています。ゼロエミッション、脱炭素を推進して経済と環境の両面で持続可能な未来を形成するためには、どのようなエネルギーが有益でしょうか。

I LISTENING

1 KEY WORD STUDY | *Before Watching the Video*

▷▷ *Match each word with its definition.*

1. accustomed ( )   2. direct debit ( )   3. efficient ( )

4. emission ( )   5. emit ( )   6. hydrogen ( )

7. longevity ( )   8. operating ( )   9. revenue ( )

10. sustainable ( )

> a. 経営上の   b. 水素   c. 排出する   d. (銀行口座) 自動引き落とし
> e. 慣れた   f. 排出物   g. 寿命   h. 持続可能な
> i. 効率的な   j. 収益

2 LISTENING PRACTICE 1 | *First Viewing*   (Time 02:21) WEB動画 🖥 DVD

▷▷ *Watch the news clip and write T if the statement is true or F if it is false.*

1. The car that hopes to bring about a green revolution is a hydrogen fuel cell vehicle. ( )

2. Riversimple is just one of the British carmakers relying solely on hydrogen fuel cell technology. ( )

3. Batteries are more suitable than hydrogen for a long-range car. ( )

4. The Rasa will enter testing with paying customers in the coming months. ( )

5. The Volkswagen Golf costs more to build than the Rasa. ( )

▷▷ *Listen to the recording and fill in the missing words.*

Narrator: The valleys of mid-Wales are a fitting home for a car that hopes to bring about a green revolution. The Rasa is a zero-emission vehicle powered not by batteries, but by a hydrogen fuel cell. It emits nothing but water vapor. The company behind it, Riversimple, is the only British carmaker relying solely on this technology. But founder Hugo Spowers believes ¹( ) ( ) ( ) ( ) ( ) over battery power.

Riversimple 英国の水素燃料車を製造する自動車会社

Hugo Spowers: A short-range car can be brilliant running on batteries, and we need them and there's a role for them, but if you want the sort of range to which we've become accustomed, of 300 miles or more, hydrogen is head and shoulders ahead ²( ) ( ) ( ) ( ) ( ) ( ).

head and shoulders ahead 〜よりずっとぬきんでて

Narrator: In the coming months the Rasa will enter testing with paying customers, one of which is Monmouthshire District Council. Their climate change officer, Jane Pratt, is taking it for a spin.

Monmouthshire District Council モンマスシャー郡議会
take 〜 for a spin 軽くドライブする
get the hang of コツを掴む

Jane Pratt: You can very quickly get the hang of it actually.

Narrator: The council have backed the project by approving a hydrogen filling station in the town of Abergavenny. It's the only one in the region, but refueling takes just minutes, ³( ) ( ) ( ) ( ) ( ). As well as the clear environmental benefit, Jane is also interested in the company's leasing model, which includes servicing and fuel costs. Riversimple still

Abergavenny 英国ウェールズ南東部のモンマスシャーにある町

owns the vehicle, and therefore has an interest in the car's longevity and efficiency.

Jane Pratt: You pay for it monthly by direct debit and everything's all under one umbrella, which I think is fantastic, and we're going to get out of this system [4](   ) (   ) (   ) (   ) and selling them and creating huge problems for ourselves for the future, whereas this is a much more sustainable method.

Narrator: Back at Riversimple's production facility, work continues to prepare for a full launch in three years' time. One of the key factors in the company's success will be the car's cost, long an Achilles heel for hydrogen power.

Achilles heel 唯一の弱点、急所

Hugo Spowers: We do expect to be able to compete with the total cost of ownership of a Golf for a customer, even though the car costs us more to build, because of these long revenue streams, and because our operating costs will be lower because the car's so efficient.

Golf フォルクスワーゲン社の小型車

Narrator: With the UK government announcing petrol and diesel engines will be phased out from 2030, the opportunity is there for hydrogen-powered cars. Riversimple hope [5](   ) (   ) (   ) (   ) (   ) (   ) will put them in pole position if it pays off.

▷▷ *Watch the news clip again and answer the following questions in English.*

1. What does a hydrogen fuel cell car emit?

   ....

2. How has Monmouthshire District Council backed the hydrogen car project?

   ....

3. What is Jane Pratt interested in?

   ....

4. What is one of the key factors in the company's success?

   ....

5. What did the UK government announce about petrol and diesel engines?

   ....

5 SUMMARY 1-32

▷▷ *Listen to the recording and complete the summary.*

The Rasa is a zero-emission vehicle powered not by batteries, but a hydrogen fuel cell. It emits nothing but water vapor. One of the key factors in the company's [1](   ) will be the car's cost, long an Achilles heel for hydrogen power. Hugo Spowers expects to be able to [2](   ) with the total cost of ownership of a Golf for a customer, even though the car costs more to build. With the UK government announcing petrol and diesel engines will be phased out from 2030, the [3](   ) is there for hydrogen-powered cars.

II READING 1-33

     In recent years, energy use and its contribution to global warming have become pressing issues. Much of the power used in machines comes from gas, oil, and coal. These fossil fuels, however, release carbon dioxide and pollutants. Countless studies have raised awareness of the harm that emissions from such fuels can do. Their

5 continued use is increasing health problems and environmental damage across the planet.

     Support for fossil fuels is due to their reliability. High levels of deposits remain unmined, and population growth has led to an increasing need for the most convenient sources of energy. Fossil fuels are cheap and widely available. Proponents

10 of the fuels say that alternative energy is more expensive to produce. They argue

that initial production costs reduce the long-term benefits. In addition, they claim that the land needed for wind or solar farms is excessive. One estimate

15 is that alternative energy production in Japan would require 2-3 percent of all the land. Furthermore, critics say that solar power is only reliable with the right level of sunlight. At the same

20 time, wind turbines, at 20 meters high, are unsightly.

But in recent years, the disadvantages of using fossil fuels have become clear. One problem is that they are non-renewable. Once used, the fuels that can take many millions of years to form are gone. Supporters of alternative energy argue that as storage technology improves, renewables will become more efficient. The diversity of

25 hydro, thermal, and biomass fuels will also provide reliability. Over time, they say, the energy will become more affordable.

Currently, renewable energy does have its drawbacks. Still, as technology advances, it is perhaps wise to strive for safer energy sources for future generations.

(281 words)

NOTES

unmined 採掘されていない   **unsightly** 目障りである

1 VOCABULARY CHECK

▷▷ *Fill in the blanks with the most appropriate word from the list below.*

1. It is natural that there is a (   ) of opinions regarding environmental issues.

2. You have to judge whether the information is (   ) when browsing the Internet.

3. This store sells organic vegetables and fruits at an (   ) price.

4. A potential (   ) of living in the city center is the high rents.

5. Kate had to take an (   ) route home due to the road closure.

drawback   diversity   reliable   alternative   affordable

2 COMPREHENSION QUESTIONS

▷ *Answer the following questions in English.*

1. What do fossil fuels release?

   ....

2. What harm do emissions from fossil fuels cause?

   ....

3. Why are fossil fuels considered the most convenient sources of energy?

   ....

4. What proportion of the land would be required to produce alternative energy in Japan?

   ....

5. What technology would improve the efficiency of alternative energy?

   ....

3 GRAMMAR CHECK

▷ *Unscramble the following words and complete the sentences.*

1. Luke became worried because [meeting, the, client, his, silent, throughout, remained].

   Luke became worried because ....

2. Helen likes pastel colors and [colors, choose, to, such, of, tends, clothes].

   Helen likes pastel colors and ....

3. Suzan's favorite sweets are [in, at, the, sold, store, front, cookies] of the station.

   Suzan's favorite sweets are .... of the station.

⫸ DISCUSSION

Alternative vs Fossil Energy: Power for the future

In September, 2020, the US State of California announced plans to ban new sales of gasoline-powered cars by 2035.

▷▷ インターネットなどを利用し、新エネルギーについて調べましょう。新エネルギーの発展や今後の可能性など良い点ばかりでなく、開発コストや環境への影響など悪い点についても検討し、下記のどちらの意見を支持するか、主張、理由など自らの考えをまとめ、発表しましょう。

Which opinion do you support and why?

A *Natural resources will run out someday, and we need to switch to alternative energy to reduce greenhouse gas emissions for the future.*

B *We have plenty of fossil fuels and we do not need to use alternative resources.*

自分の意見

理由

REFERENCES

再生可能エネルギー
太陽光・風力・地熱・中小水力・バイオマスといった再生可能エネルギーは、温室効果ガスを排出せず、国内で生産できることから、エネルギー安全保障にも寄与できる有望かつ多様で、重要な低炭素の国際エネルギー源である。

経済産業省資源エネルギー庁「再生可能エネルギーとは」https://www.enecho.meti.go.jp/category/saving_and_new/saiene/renewable/outline/index.html

Vegetarians vs Meat Eaters:
Fighting dietary habits for the environment

気候変動への影響から食習慣を見直す人々が見受けられます。菜食主義と肉食では、健康や環境に良いのはどちらでしょうか。環境への影響を視点に、食習慣について議論しましょう。

◢ LISTENING

1 KEY WORD STUDY | *Before Watching the Video*

▷▷ *Match each word with its definition.*

1. aspiring ( )　　2. compensate ( )　　3. consistency ( )

4. consumption ( )　　5. dairy ( )　　6. ecology ( )

7. nutrient ( )　　8. protein ( )　　9. tricky ( )

10. vegetarian ( )

> a. 野心のある　　b. 生態学　　c. 消費　　d. 一貫性
>
> e. 補う　　f. 乳製品　　g. タンパク質　　h. 菜食主義者
>
> i. 栄養素　　j. 扱いにくい

2 LISTENING PRACTICE 1 | *First Viewing* (Time 02:42) WEB動画 📺 DVD

▷▷ *Watch the news clip and write T if the statement is true or F if it is false.*

1. Christophe Lomet doesn't care about the kind of food he buys. ( )

2. Christophe Lomet is asking everyone to become vegan. ( )

3. In Lyon, France, being vegan is considered very important. ( )

4. Dr Arnaud Cocaul agrees that consuming less meat is better for the environment.

　( )

5. Reducing food waste is a simple way to limit the environmental impact of food production. ( )

3 LISTENING PRACTICE 2

 2-02

▷▷ *Listen to the recording and fill in the missing words.*

Narrator: When it comes to reducing his impact on the planet and its resources, Christophe Lomet has a simple solution. An aspiring businessman, Christophe is careful about which food he buys and what goes on his plate.

Christophe Lomet: Well, I'm vegan and that's also one of the reasons [1](　　　)(　　　)(　　　) (　　　)(　　　)(　　　) (　　　)(　　　). For most foods here the carbon footprint is very low. There's no meat, they don't sell any at the moment and so I'd rather support a business like this.

carbon footprint 二酸化炭素排出量

Narrator: Tonight, Christophe is cooking for friends who've cut back on their meat consumption. A look in their fridge is encouraging for Christophe.

Christophe Lomet: There's a lot of dairy and vegan products. Which means that Bryce and Lucien are trying to be reasonable in terms of their food and I think that's great, pretty cool. I'm not asking everyone to become vegan, unfortunately.

Narrator: It's time to prepare the evening meal, a vegan shepherd's pie, with soy protein replacing the meat. For Christophe, [2](　　　)(　　　) (　　　)(　　　)(　　　) or no carbon footprint.

shepherd's pie シェパード[羊飼いの]（牛肉とポテトの）パイ

Christophe Lomet: I think that ecology is really the best way to convince people to adopt vegetable-based diets. We try to talk about greenhouse gas emissions and the energy consumption involved in producing meat or dairy food.

Narrator: A little malted yeast on the mashed potatoes, in the oven for 20 minutes [3](   ) (   ) (   ) (   ).

Bryce: Bon appétit.

Narrator: But is it to everyone's liking?

Lucien: Well, the consistency is pretty good.

Bryce: And the spices make up for the lack of meat.

Narrator: Christophe's friends are not quite ready to follow in his footsteps.

Lucien: Socially, it's tricky. I know a vegetarian who became vegan then switched back because of that, and [4](   ) (   ) (   ) (   ) (   ). I'm from Lyon, where food is considered very important and is far from being vegan.

Narrator: Doctor Arnaud Cocaul is a nutritionist who agrees that eating less meat is better for the environment. But not at the expense of crucial nutrients.

Dr Arnaud Cocaul: A diet which is good for the planet isn't necessarily good for your body. So I think we have to be very careful. If you want to give up animal protein, you have to be sure you're compensating for it with vegetable protein.

Narrator: One simple way to limit the impact our food production and choices make on the planet is fighting waste. One-point-three billion tons of food [5](   ) (   ) (   ) (   ) (   ) every year, the equivalent of one third of global food production.

Bon appétit 召し上がれ

Lyon リヨン（フランス中東部にある同国第3の都市）

4 COMPREHENSION CHECK | *Second Viewing*

▷▷ *Watch the news clip again and answer the following questions in English.*

1. Why does Christophe Lomet come to the shop?

   ....

2. For who does Christophe Lomet cook on that night?

   ....

3. What is the meat replaced with in a vegan shepherd's pie?

   ....

4. What does Christophe Lomet think is the best way to convince people to adopt a vegetable-based diet?

   ....

5. What is Dr Cocaul's advice regarding giving up animal protein?

   ....

5 SUMMARY

 2-03

▷▷ *Listen to the recording and complete the summary.*

When it comes to reducing his impact on the planet and its resources, Christophe Lomet has a simple solution. He is careful about which food he buys and what goes on his plate. He is cooking for friends who have cut back on their meat [1](   ). Doctor Arnaud Cocaul is a nutritionist who agrees that consuming less meat is better for the [2](   ). One simple way to limit the impact our food production and choices make on the planet is fighting waste. One-point-three billion tons of food are lost or thrown away every year, the [3](   ) of one third of global food production.

⚋⚋ READING

 2-04

Research suggests that a vegetarian diet has many advantages. There are two broad types of vegetarian. Those who refrain from eating meat but may eat dairy or seafood. And others, who, in addition to not eating meat, also avoid all animal by-products such as leather or honey. However, meat-eaters strongly disagree that this is
5 the only form of diet that can be viewed as healthy or ethical.

Those who reject the vegetarian diet argue that eating meat is innate. They say that modern methods rear animals without cruelty or drug use, and their slaughter is humane. Secondly, they argue that no study has linked beyond doubt eating meat with a higher risk of contracting illnesses such as heart disease. Thirdly, they claim that vegetarian diets do not always protect nature. Growing single crops, they say, erodes the topsoil that contains nutrients for plants to survive. Lastly, they insist that vegetarians do not live longer. They highlight studies that found no significant differences in death rates.

However, vegetarians dispute these points. They argue that eating meat is not natural at all. They say that ignoring other food sources is cruel and that animals are not all well reared. Secondly, they point out extensive studies showing that vegetarians are less likely to die from heart-related problems or to develop diabetes or cancer. Thirdly, they argue that animal overgrazing harms the environment while a plant-based diet saves water and reduces air pollution. Lastly, they say that several large-scale studies have proven the link between a plant-based diet and longevity.

The arguments suggest that a vegetarian diet is wholly beneficial. But it will take time to convince most people who enjoy eating meat to reconsider their choices.

(284 words)

NOTES

rear 飼育する   **topsoil** 表土   **overgrazing** 過放牧

1 | VOCABULARY CHECK

▷▷ *Fill in the blanks with the most appropriate word from the list below.*

1. The committee has decided to (   ) the plan from scratch.
2. The shoreline will continue to (   ), eventually transforming the landscape of the area.
3. The companies were able to reach an agreement (   ) for both parties.
4. What counts as an (   ) decision can greatly differ between cultures.
5. Animals are born with an (   ) ability to find food sources.

> ethical   beneficial   innate   erode   reconsider

2 COMPREHENSION QUESTIONS

▷▷ *Answer the following questions in English.*

1. What do those who follow a strict type of vegetarian diet avoid in addition to meat?

    ....

2. What do people who oppose a vegetarian diet argue regarding eating meat?

    ....

3. What is a potential risk of growing single crops?

    ....

4. What illnesses are vegetarians less likely to have?

    ....

5. How is a plant-based diet environmentally friendly?

    ....

3 GRAMMAR CHECK

▷▷ *Unscramble the following words and complete the sentences.*

1. You should [talking, on, from, the, refrain, phone] on the train in Japan.

    You should .... on the train in Japan.

2. Some people think that there is not enough evidence [warming, emission, CO_2, global, link, with, the, to, of].

    Some people think that there is not enough evidence ....

    ....

3. My teacher [sign, convinced, has, to, up, me] for the project.

    My teacher .... for the project.

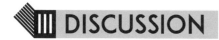 **DISCUSSION**

Vegetarians vs Meat Eaters:
Fighting dietary habits for the environment.

There are a number of debates about vegetarianism and eating meat to create a sustainable environment.

▷▷ インターネットなどを利用し、肉食が環境に与える影響について調べましょう。肉食が健康のために必要な良い点ばかりでなく、肉食用の家畜の飼育が及ぼす環境への負荷など悪い点についても検討し、下記のどちらの意見を支持するか、主張、理由など自らの考えをまとめ、発表しましょう。

Which opinion do you support and why?

A *I would like to be a vegetarian because animal farming is not good for the environment.*

B *I would prefer to eat meat because animal farming does not pollute the environment.*

自分の意見 _____

理由

_____

_____

_____

_____

REFERENCES

A

畜産が及ぼす環境への影響

畜産によって排出される温室効果ガスは、乗り物が排出するガス量よりはるかに多く、世界の水資源の3分の1もが畜産業のために消費されている。アマゾン森林破壊は91%が畜産業による。

Ethical Choice「畜産と環境問題」2020年12月 https://myethicalchoice.com/journal/climate-change/livestock-and-environment/

B

肉を食べることの利点

肉を食べることは、人が健康に生きるために大切であり、たんぱく質は筋肉や臓器などをつくる材料になる。肉などの動物性たんぱく質は、骨を作るメカニズムを促進しホルモンのバランスを整える効果もある。赤身の肉を適正量食べている限り、脂肪過多になったりコレステロールが高くなったりすることはない。

エバラ食品「お肉の参考書」2019年4月 https://www.ebarafoods.com/sp/meat/health/

Endangered Species vs Diplomacy: Animal rights

国と国との友好関係を築き、維持するために、自国の希少動物を相手国に寄贈することがあります。希少動物の種の保護と外交は、どちらを優先させるべきでしょうか。

I LISTENING

1 KEY WORD STUDY | *Before Watching the Video*

▷▷ *Match each word with its definition.*

1. administration (　)　　2. benevolence　(　)　　3. breeding　(　)
4. in captivity　(　)　　5. clan　　　　　(　)　　6. diplomacy　(　)
7. endangered　(　)　　8. generosity　　(　)　　9. maturity　　(　)
10. pregnant　(　)

> a. 飼育下で　　b. 絶滅の危機に瀕した　　c. 寛大さ　　d. 妊娠している
> e. 外交　　　　f. 政権　　　　　　　　g. 成熟　　　h. 繁殖
> i. 慈悲心　　　j. 仲間

2 LISTENING PRACTICE 1 | *First Viewing*　　　　(Time 02:30) WEB動画 📺 DVD

▷▷ *Watch the news clip and write T if the statement is true or F if it is false.*

1. Bei Bei will be sent to the Washington National Zoo and is spending his final days in Beijing. (　)
2. Bei Bei was born on August 22, 2015 in Beijing. (　)
3. Fifteen to 20 kilos of bamboo will be taken with Bei Bei for his 16-hour flight. (　)
4. Panda diplomacy between China and the US began with Richard Nixon's visit to Beijing in 1972. (　)
5. Bei Bei's parents were donated to the Clinton administration in 2020. (　)

▷▷ *Listen to the recording and fill in the missing words.*

Narrator: It's the end of an era for Bei Bei. The giant panda is spending his final days at the Washington National Zoo, before boarding a one-way flight to Beijing. His American fans ¹( ) ( ) ( ) ( ).

Linda Knippers: We love Bei Bei. We discovered him when he was about six months old through the panda cam, and since then we've been coming fairly regularly  to see him. And I just wanted to come for our last opportunity before he goes to China.

Hope Endrenyi: I'm sad that we don't get to see him anymore, but I'm happy he's going back to his homeland. I'm sure he'll be happy ²( ) ( ) ( ) ( ) ( ) as well.

Narrator: Bei Bei, which means "precious treasure" in Mandarin, was born from artificial insemination on August 22, 2015, here in the US capital. But according to the agreement between Beijing and the National Zoo, he —like his brothers and sisters before him—must be returned to China after his fourth birthday.

Marty Dearie: We'll probably be taking 15 or 20 kilos of bamboo with him at least. He'll also get ³( ),  ( ) ( ), ( ). We'll probably take some sugar cane, there might be honey, biscuits. All the things that he kind of likes throughout the day here, we're going to take with him, so that on that 16-hour flight, we can provide him with everything that he needs.

Bei Bei ベイベイ(貝貝)パンダ の名前
the Washington National Zoo 国立動物園

Mandarin 北京官話(中国の 標準語)
artificial insemination 人工 授精

Narrator: "Panda diplomacy" between China and the US dates back to Richard Nixon's historic visit to Beijing in 1972. Then-prime minister Zhou Enlai gifted him a pair of pandas. Since then, [4]( ) ( ) ( ) ( ) ( ) has continued with the US and elsewhere. Once the pandas reach sexual maturity, they become part of a breeding program back in China. Bei Bei's parents, given to the Clinton administration, are on loan until December 2020. These valuable tenants cost the zoo half a million dollars a year.

Richard Nixon 第37代米国合衆国大統領(1969-74)

Zhou Enlai 周恩来

Clinton Bill Clinton. 第42代米国合衆国大統領(1993-2001)

Liselotte Odgaard: It's a symbol of China's history, its benevolence, generosity, etc. So especially at the moment when you hear so many negative stories about China, they [5]( ) ( ) ( ) ( ) ( ) ( ) ( ) counter-move to that, and to sort of make the general public think well of China.

Narrator: Giant pandas are an endangered species, with only 1,800 living in the wild and 500 in captivity worldwide. The Washington Zoo will have to wait for Bei Bei's mother to get pregnant for a fourth time before another panda can join its clan.

4 COMPREHENSION CHECK | *Second Viewing*

▷▷ *Watch the news clip again and answer the following questions in English.*

1. How old was Bei Bei when Linda Knippers discovered him for the first time through the panda cam?

   ....

2. How does Hope Endrenyi feel about Bei Bei's going to China?

   ....

3. Why must Bei Bei be returned to China?

   ....

4. How much a year did it cost the National Zoo to borrow Bei Bei's parents?

   ....

5. Altogether, how many giant pandas are living in the wild and in zoos worldwide?

   ....

5 SUMMARY

 2-07

▷▷ *Listen to the recording and complete the summary.*

The giant panda is spending his final days at the Washington National Zoo, before boarding a one-way flight to Beijing. "Panda diplomacy" between China and the US dates back to Richard Nixon's [1]( ) visit to Beijing in 1972. So especially at the moment, when there are so many [2]( ) stories about China, the country is using the panda as a sort of counter-move, and to make the general public think well of it. The Washington Zoo will have to wait for Bei Bei's mother to get [3]( ) for a fourth time before another panda joins its clan.

II READING

 2-08

Known as "Panda Diplomacy," sending giant pandas overseas as a gesture of friendship was first recorded in the year 685. In China, pandas are "national treasures" and are revered as part of an ancient culture. However, their status is listed as "vulnerable." This is mainly due to the loss of bamboo forests and poaching.
5 Ostensibly, pandas are loaned to countries worldwide as part of a breeding program. Countries work together to learn more about them. But there is more to the loan practice than simple preservation.

China uses pandas as part of its international diplomacy. As they are rare
10 creatures, sending them to other countries can improve China's caring image. Zoos often prepare special enclosures at a high cost, and the animals frequently become a favorite with visitors. In addition,
15 presenting such popular animals to

foreign countries can help with trade talks. It also aids in negotiations for resources or technology. Governments defend panda loans saying they benefit everyone by developing good relationships.

But some have questioned the use of such vulnerable animals for diplomacy.
20 Although pandas are no longer endangered, they still behave very differently in zoos than in the wild. Research suggests that problems with breeding occur more often in captivity. And they argue that a zoo with crowds of onlookers is a stressful environment for the pandas. Some also claim that there are better ways to help them. They say China should seek to safeguard their natural habitat, not send them
25 overseas.

Both views have their merits. It is vital to develop good global relations, exchange research, and allow people worldwide to see such beautiful creatures. Still, care must be taken to protect and preserve, not harm, and exploit them.

(284 words)

NOTES

revered 尊敬される **ostensibly** 表向きは

1 VOCABULARY CHECK

▷▷ *Fill in the blanks with the most appropriate word from the list below.*

1. The (   ) of polar bears is limited to the Arctic.

2. Lucy saw a (   ) which looked like a bear on her way home from school.

3. Mason had to teach his dog how to (   ) when someone new visits his house.

4. Records show that cats were worshipped in (   ) Egypt.

5. Developed countries have a responsibility to (   ) developing countries.

ancient   habitat   aid   behave   creature

2 COMPREHENSION QUESTIONS

▷▷ *Answer the following questions in English.*

1. In what year were giant pandas first sent overseas as a gesture of friendship?

    ....

2. Why are pandas currently listed as a vulnerable species?

    ....

3. What kind of image of the country can China generate by sending pandas to other countries?

    ....

4. Why are zoos potentially a stressful environment for pandas?

    ....

5. What do skeptics say China should do instead of sending pandas overseas?

    ....

3 GRAMMAR CHECK

▷▷ *Unscramble the following words and complete the sentences.*

1. Our local [often, events, zoo, special, more, holds] these days in order to attract new visitors.

    Our local .... these days in order to attract new visitors.

2. The musical was cancelled after the first part [actor, injury, to, of, the, the, main, due].

    The musical was cancelled after the first part ....

    ....

3. The stand [food, sell, in, to, to, addition, started] bubble tea.

    The stand .... bubble tea.

 DISCUSSION

Endangered Species vs Diplomacy: Animal rights

Animals have been used as diplomatic gifts for centuries.

▷▷ インターネットなどを利用し、動物外交について調べましょう。動物外交による国家間の交流や外交関係の進展など良い点ばかりでなく、種の保護への影響など悪い点についても検討し、下記のどちらの意見を支持するか、主張、理由など自らの考えをまとめ、発表しましょう。

Which opinion do you support and why?

A *Giving endangered species as gifts to other countries is a good form of diplomacy.*

B *Endangered species should be protected and not used for diplomacy.*

自分の意見 _____

理由

_____
_____
_____
_____

REFERENCES

A

パンダ外交
ワシントン条約によりレンタル扱い
現在ではワシントン条約とその加盟国が独自に条約運用のために定めた法の影響で学術研究目的以外での取引は難しいため、外交として中国国外にジャイアントパンダを贈与することはできず、中国の動物園か保護センターで生まれた個体を「繁殖・研究」などの名目で中国国外の動物園にレンタルする形となっており、レンタルされる個体はすべて「中国籍」である。

B

希少な野生生物の保護
現在、世界では数多くの野生生物が、開発や人が持ち込んだ外来生物、乱獲、地球温暖化などにより、絶滅の危機に瀕している。IUCN（国際自然保護連合）がまとめた、「レッドリスト」には、絶滅のおそれの高い種として、1万6,000種あまりの動植物がリストアップされている。
WWF 2009年9月 https://www.wwf.or.jp/activities/wildlife/

Old vs New Industries: Solving unemployment

米国の Rust Belt 地域のように、英国の Ebbw Vale はかつて炭鉱や鉄鋼業で発展しました。地域産業の衰退とともに失業者が増え、経済再生の対策が期待されています。どのような政策が地域再生のために効果的でしょうか。

I LISTENING

1 KEY WORD STUDY | *Before Watching the Video*

▷▷ *Match each word with its definition.*

1. chuck ( )   2. disapproval ( )   3. funding ( )

4. investment ( )   5. regional ( )   6. symbolize ( )

7. transition ( )   8. unemployment ( )   9. vocational college ( )

10. wasteful ( )

> a. 専門学校   b. 象徴化する   c. 移行   d. 投資
> e. 失業   f. 投げる   g. 無駄な   h. 不賛成
> i. 地方の   j. 資金

2 LISTENING PRACTICE 1 | *First Viewing*   (Time 02:03)   WEB動画   DVD

▷▷ *Watch the news clip and write T if the statement is true or F if it is false.*

1. Ebbw Vale was the home of the largest steelworks in Europe until 2002. ( )

2. Mark Davis thinks the UK government needs to change its way of thinking. ( )

3. The UK government has paid for road and rail links and other projects in Ebbw Vale. ( )

4. The redevelopment project of the town square is considered a symbol of useful EU spending. ( )

5. An eye-catching project built with EU funds has been widely accepted. ( )

3 | LISTENING PRACTICE 2

WEB動画 DVD CD 2-10

▷▷ *Listen to the recording and fill in the missing words.*

Narrator: The valley of Ebbw Vale used to be home to the largest steelworks in Europe. But production ended in 2002, ¹( ) ( ) ( ) ( ) ( ) ( ) ( ). Since then, hundreds of millions of euros have been poured into the area by the European Regional Development Fund—investment which will end now the UK has left the EU. But locals hope the British government will step in to fill the vacuum.

| Ebbw Vale 英国ウェールズの都市 |

| European Regional Development Fund ヨーロッパ地域開発基金(EU内の開発途上地域や衰退産業をかかえる地域での開発計画に対し無償援助を行うことを目的に設立された基金) |

Mark Davis: I think the government needs to change its way of thinking, that the EU will not be there to chuck money at us that we can actually use, we have to find our own way of doing it, and the only way that can happen is ²( ) ( ) ( ) ( ) ( ) smaller areas like this and realizes that the investment is needed.

Narrator: Over the years the EU has paid for road and rail links, sports facilities, and educational projects like this adult learning center. But despite this, the area saw the highest pro-Brexit vote in all of Wales. ³( ) ( ) ( ) ( ) has come to represent local disapproval of the EU. A symbol of Wales, for many here, this town square redevelopment project also symbolizes wasteful EU spending, an eye-catching project which didn't directly create jobs.

| pro-Brexit 英国のEU離脱に賛成 |
| Wales ウェールズ |

Rowenn Ogunfimbo: The decoration that they've used the funds for hasn't been that widely accepted, and I think the rest of us just think it is a waste of money.

Narrator: More practical EU projects include this vocational college, built on the site of the former steelworks. High-school students learn practical design and engineering skills here. Staff at the center worry that [4]( ) ( ) ( ) ( ) ( ) European support.

Dan Coles: I suspect that there will be less funding available to us so we are going to have to be a lot more focused about what we do, and what those benefits will be.

Narrator: Boris Johnson's government has pledged to "level-up" parts of the UK that are in the economic slow lane. But it may prove a difficult promise to keep if the economy suffers following the post-Brexit transition, [5]( ) ( ) ( ) ( ) ( ) ( ).

Boris Johnson 第77代イギリス首相

post-Brexit 英国のEU離脱後

4 COMPREHENSION CHECK | *Second Viewing*

WEB動画 DVD

▷▷ *Watch the news clip again and answer the following questions in English.*

1. Which organization has poured investment into Ebbw Vale?

   ....

2. How did the people in Ebbw Vale vote in the referendum on Brexit?

   ....

3. What do more practical EU projects include?

   ....

4. What does Dan Coles suspect about the funding?

   ....

5. What has Boris Johnson's government pledged?

   ....

5 SUMMARY

 2-11

▷▷ *Listen to the recording and complete the summary.*

Since 2002, hundreds of millions of euros have been poured into Ebbw Vale by the European Regional Development Fund, but locals hope the British government will step in to fill the [1]( ). Over the years the EU has paid for road and rail links, sports facilities, and educational projects like this adult learning center. But despite this, the area saw the highest pro-Brexit vote in all of Wales. Boris Johnson's government has [2]( ) to "level-up" parts of the UK that are in the economic slow lane. But it may prove a difficult promise to keep if the economy [3]( ) following the post-Brexit transition.

READING

 2-12

Global warming has drawn attention to issues facing traditional businesses. Economies must confront changes in the job market amid less demand for "blue-collar" workers. As a result of job losses, towns and cities fade, and there is fierce debate about how to revive them. Some say it will only happen with more forward-
5 thinking investment in the training and job sectors. Others argue for upgrading infrastructure to protect jobs. Governments must choose whether to support more climate-friendly businesses or put more money into what many believe to be waning industries.

  Studies suggest large manufacturing and production firms often rely on
10 unsustainable models. Gas, food, and coal mining firms are known as significant sources of CO_2 emissions. The companies typically employ great numbers of workers who can suffer social
15 and economic hardship when they close. The loss of such large firms can devastate towns. Many claim that these businesses are worth saving.
20 With better investment, they say, a company can upgrade

to "clean" methods and, in doing so, help restore local communities.

On the other hand, new industries adopt the latest technology and rely less on natural resources. Many believe that it would be wrong to invest in emission-producing businesses, even to revive a town and provide jobs. They refer to coal mining as an example. Despite large increases in funding, the industry continues polluting. Instead, they argue for new businesses to revive towns. These might include solar power, organic farming, or recycling. They claim that this would make the best use of often highly skilled workers.

Future investment must account for the climate. Retraining, education, and sustainable businesses may be the best answer to revive areas in decline and put new life into local communities.

(284 words)

NOTES

waning 衰えていく　**devastate** 荒廃させる

1 VOCABULARY CHECK

▷▷ *Fill in the blanks with the most appropriate word from the list below.*

1. Charlie decided to (　　　　　) his boss about the unpaid salary at his part-time job.
2. There has been (　　　　　) competition between mobile phone service providers.
3. The company decided to (　　　　　) the old action game because it was likely to appeal to the customer base.
4. Sunlight causes the paintings to (　　　　　) over the course of time.
5. Joel prefers to buy (　　　　　) vegetables because he is worried about pesticide residues.

organic　　fierce　　fade　　revive　　confront

78

2 COMPREHENSION QUESTIONS

▷▷ *Answer the following questions in English.*

1. What do governments have to decide when they support businesses?

   ....

2. Which industries are known as significant sources of CO_2 emissions?

   ....

3. With better investment, how can traditional firms change?

   ....

4. What do new industries tend to adopt?

   ....

5. What could be the best answer to revive areas in decline?

   ....

3 GRAMMAR CHECK

▷▷ *Unscramble the following words and complete the sentences.*

1. The new documentary series [is, on, watching, change, worth, climate]
   repeatedly.

   The new documentary series ....
   repeatedly.

2. [students, number, showed, a, of, interest, large] in participating in the event.

   .... in participating in the event.

3. Ms. Anderson refused to think about the scenario [of, for, the, argument, even,
   sake].

   Ms. Anderson refused to think about the scenario ....
   ....

DISCUSSION

Old vs New Industries: Solving unemployment

With the decline of American manufacturing since 2000, what are better solutions for saving "rust belt" cities?

▷ インターネットなどを利用し、地域再生について調べましょう。新たな産業の誘致や今後の可能性、失業者対策、かつての産業の再生策なども検討し、下記のどちらの意見を支持するか、主張、理由など自らの考えをまとめ、発表しましょう。

Which opinion do you support and why?

A *We need to create new industries to solve unemployment problems and help revive deserted towns.*

B *Going back to old industries will help revive deserted towns.*

自分の意見 _____

理由

_____
_____
_____
_____

REFERENCES

ラスト・ベルト

　米国中西部地域と大西洋岸中部地域の一部の領域（イリノイ、インディアナ、ミシガン、オハイオ、ペンシルバニア諸州の一部）を表現する呼称で、米国経済の重工業と製造業の重要な部分を形成している。

　この領域は古くからウエストバージニア州やテネシー州、ケンタッキー州及びペンシルベニア州の石炭や五大湖の水運を活かし製造業と重工業の中心となり、シカゴ、クリーブランド、バッファロー、デトロイトおよびトレドは五大湖の主要港として栄えてきたが、1970 年代以降国際競争への対応策として製造業者がメキシコ等海外に転出し、米国の製造業が衰退していくのに伴い、これを強調するラストベルト（錆の帯）という別名が付いた。

　米国の製造業は労働集約型の生産工程では中国等の低賃金国には勝てないため、高付加価値製品の生産と先進的無人化生産方式に移行し、米国の製造業は雇用は減少している生産量は増加しており、ラストベルトはその中心となっている。

投資用語集「ラストベルト」https://www.glossary.jp/econ/economy/rust-belt.php

LESSON 12

Needed vs Not Needed:
Affirmative action

男女共同参画・積極的差別是正
措置が推進されていますが、ガラス
天井など見えない差別はいまだに存
在しているようです。一方、積極的
差別是正措置は逆差別であるという
意見も聞かれます。平等な社会とは、
どのようなものでしょうか。

I LISTENING

1 KEY WORD STUDY | *Before Watching the Video*

▷▷ *Match each word with its definition.*

1. attorney   (　)   2. bid   (　)   3. controversy   (　)

4. immigrant   (　)   5. judiciary   (　)   6. overhaul   (　)

7. presidency   (　)   8. proclaim   (　)   9. high-profile   (　)

10. reckoning   (　)

a. 大統領職	b. 論争	c. 司法	d. 検事
e. 移民	f. 見直す	g. 宣言する	h. 注目度の高い
i. 報い	j. 立候補		

2 LISTENING PRACTICE 1 | *First Viewing*   (Time 01:59) 🖥 WEB動画 💿 DVD

▷▷ *Watch the news clip and write T if the statement is true or F if it is false.*

1. Kamala Harris is America's next Vice President and has a history of firsts. (　)

2. Harris became the first Black Governor of California in 2016.   (　)

3. Harris marched with protesters after the police killing of George Floyd in 2020.

(　)

4. Harris thinks that America is in the midst of a reckoning on financial injustice.

(　)

5. Harris has promised to be a team player in the Biden administration.   (　)

WEB動画 DVD CD 2-14

▷▷ *Listen to the recording and fill in the missing words.*

Kamala Harris: But while I may be the first woman in this office, I will not be the last.

I will not be the last.

Narrator: America's next Vice President, Kamala Harris, has a history of firsts.

Kamala Harris: We did it, Joe. You're going to be [1](   )
(   ) (   ) (   )
(   ) (   ) (   ).

Joe Joe Biden. 第46代米国合衆国大統領 (2021-)

Narrator: She is the first woman of color to be elected as VP. Before that, she was the first Black female district attorney of San Francisco, and then state Attorney General. In 2016, she became the first Black senator from California. Harris has held seats on several high-profile committees, including Intelligence and Judiciary. She's known [2](   ) (   ) (   )
(   ) (   ) (   ).

Attorney General 司法長官

senator 上院議員

Kamala Harris: Is he fit to be a jurist?

Narrator: To Democratic voters, Harris is a familiar face; running against Joe Biden [3](   ) (   )
(   ) (   ) (   )
(   ) for the presidency in the 2020 race. Born in Oakland, the 56-year-old is the daughter of two immigrants, an Indian mother and a father from Jamaica. Known as "Momala" to her step-children, she is married to lawyer Doug Emhoff, who will become the first Second Gentleman. Harris [4](   ) (   )
(   ) (   ) (   )
(   ) Howard University in Washington, DC. She marched with protesters after the police killing of George Floyd in 2020 and she's supported proposals to

Democratic 民主党の

Second Gentleman 副大統領の夫

George Floyd
2020年5月25日に米国合衆国ミネソタ州ミネアポリスで逮捕される最中に警官に死亡させられたアフリカ系アメリカ人

overhaul policing.

Kamala Harris: We are in the midst of a long-overdue reckoning on racial injustice in America.

Narrator: Her path to the Vice Presidency has not been without controversy. [5](   ) (   ) (   ) (   ) her tough line during her time as California Attorney General. And she served in the Senate for less than one term before seeking higher office. But Harris—a self-proclaimed fan of hip hop—has promised to be a team player in the Biden administration, and work in lockstep with the incoming President.

Senate 上院

lockstep 決まりきったやり方

4 COMPREHENSION CHECK | *Second Viewing*

▷▷ *Watch the news clip again and answer the following questions in English.*

1. What was Kamala Harris before she was elected as Vice President?
   ....

2. What high-profile committee seats has Harris held?
   ....

3. Where was Harris born and where did her parents come from?
   ....

4. Who will become the first Second Gentleman?
   ....

5. How long did Harris serve in the Senate before seeking higher office?
   ....

5 SUMMARY

 2-15

▷▷ *Listen to the recording and complete the summary.*

Kamala Harris crashed through one of the world's highest glass ceilings to be elected America's first woman Vice President, making history and helping bring to an end Donald Trump's [1](   ) presidency. By winning the Vice Presidency, she will be a heartbeat away from leading the United States and poised on a stepping-stone to the [2](   ) prize. Harris was born to immigrants to the United States—her father from Jamaica, her mother from India—and their lives and her own have in some ways [3](   ) the American dream.

 # ⁐ READING 2-16

Affirmative action means that preferential treatment is given to minorities. Quotas may be applied in areas such as employment or higher education. Supporters claim quotas provide more equal opportunities and promote social diversity. In theory, it appears fair to use such measures to raise equality. However, as the benefits
5　are a matter of opinion, the practice is keenly debated.

Those against quotas argue that it weakens meritocracy. This system, they say, allows those with the strongest abilities to rise to the top and fulfill their potential. They believe it is good for society that those with talent reach leadership positions. They claim that allowing quotas is biased against those from other backgrounds.
10　It does not work, they argue, because more highly qualified applicants lose out. They may be turned down in favor of those with fewer skills or lower test scores. In addition, they say that a person given a position because of quotas does not gain the same respect as a person who has earned it.

Those in favor of quotas argue that it compensates for social inequalities faced
15　by minorities. Supporters say that meritocracies do not allow chances for everyone. In truth, they sustain inequality. Studies show that minorities continue to be underrepresented in all areas of society. As a result, quotas are a valuable tool for promoting social mobility. Greater access to higher education, for example, gives more opportunities for minorities to succeed. In addition, supporters believe that diversity
20　can enrich everyone. They say that being around others helps people relate more.

Affirmative action is not the final answer to inequality. However, while disparities continue to exist, quotas may help ensure that every person is given a fair chance.

(282 words)

NOTES

quota 割り当て　　**meritocracy** 能力主義

1 VOCABULARY CHECK

▷▷ *Fill in the blanks with the most appropriate word from the list below.*

1. Continuous learning can (　　　　　　) people's lives because it is never too late to learn something new.
2. Oliver worked eagerly in order to (　　　　　　) for his lack of experience in the sector.

3. It is undeniable that there are economic (   ) between developed countries and developing countries.

4. You need to have at least three years of teaching experience in order to (   ) for this position.

5. More (   ) have to be taken in order to protect the copyright of publications.

measures   enrich   disparities   qualify   compensate

2 COMPREHENSION QUESTIONS

▷▷ *Answer the following questions in English.*

1. In which areas is affirmative action implemented?

   ....

2. Why do some people believe that meritocracy is good for society?

   ....

3. What do studies show regarding the representation of minorities in society?

   ....

4. What opportunities can access to higher education provide for minorities?

   ....

5. What can affirmative action help to ensure?

   ....

3 GRAMMAR CHECK

▷▷ *Unscramble the following words and complete the sentences.*

1. Students were [rules, introduction, of, the, against, new, the] on club activities on campus.

   Students were .... on club activities on campus.

2. In the end, [the, the, of, in, was, ruling, prosecutors, court, favor].

   In the end, ...

3. Some people prefer outdoor activities, [home, to, and, while, prefer, others, stay] relax.

   Some people prefer outdoor activities, ... relax.

Needed vs Not Needed: Affirmative action

Affirmative action refers to a set of policies and practices within a government or organization seeking to include particular groups based on their gender, race, sexuality, creed, or nationality in areas in which they are underrepresented, such as education and employment.

▷▷ インターネットなどを利用し、男女共同参画・積極的格差是正措置について調べましょう。社会における平等の可能性など良い点ばかりでなく、逆差別の影響など悪い点についても検討し、下記のどちらの意見を支持するか、主張、理由など自らの考えをまとめ、発表しましょう。

Which opinion do you support and why?

◣ **A** *Affirmative action is needed to help minorities.*

◣ **B** *Affirmative action is not needed because you can succeed in society if you have talent or money or are smart.*

自分の意見 _____

理由

_____

_____

_____

REFERENCES

A	B
アファーマティブアクション (affirmative action) 日本語では「積極的格差是正措置」や「肯定的措置」と訳される言葉である。社会的・構造的な差別によって不利益を被っている者に対し、一定の範囲で特別の機会を提供することにより、実質的な機会均等を実現することを目的とする措置のことを言う。 ELEMINIST「アファーマティブアクションとは？」2020 年 10 月 https://eleminist.com/article/497	**アファーマティブアクションの問題点 逆差別の助長** アファーマティブアクションでは、社会的に差別を受けてきた弱者に対し、その格差を是正するための優遇措置を実施するケースが多くみられる。マイノリティに対する救済として優遇措置は行われるが、その度合いによってはマジョリティに対する差別、つまり「逆差別」と言われかねない状況も引き起こすのだ。 ELEMINIST「アファーマティブアクションとは？」2020 年 10 月 https://eleminist.com/article/497

Traditional vs Innovative: Food culture you prefer

日本の洋食、ハワイアンフュージョン料理、TEXMEX など世界にはさまざまな食文化の融合があります。伝統的な食文化の継承と革新的な食文化の創造では、どちらが大切でしょうか。また、あなたはどちらを好みますか。

I LISTENING

1 | KEY WORD STUDY | *Before Watching the Video*

▷▷ *Match each word with its definition.*

1. distort	( )	2. entrepreneur	( )	3. expand	( )
4. fatty	( )	5. hectic	( )	6. ingredient	( )
7. mellow	( )	8. perch	( )	9. recipe	( )
10. renowned	( )				

> a. 脂ののった   b. ゆがめる   c. 調理法   d. 高い場所に作る
> e. 熟成した   f. 大忙しの   g. 起業家   h. 広げる
> i. 原料   j. 有名な

2 | LISTENING PRACTICE 1 | *First Viewing* (Time 02:24) WEB動画 📺 DVD

▷▷ *Watch the news clip and write T if the statement is true or F if it is false.*

1. Lalaina Ravelomanana is a world-famous chef. ( )
2. He likes mixing caviar with salmon. ( )
3. Madagascan caviar is sold for 750 euros per kilo and is more expensive than the French caviar. ( )
4. Gray is a good color for caviar. ( )
5. Lake Mantasoa has very pure water and no commercial activity around it. ( )

WEB動画 DVD CD 2-18

▷▷ *Listen to the recording and fill in the missing words.*

Narrator: It's another hectic day in the kitchen at this high-end restaurant in Antananarivo. Locally renowned chef Lalaina Ravelomanana is creating new recipes, to take advantage of Madagascar's own caviar, the first to be produced in Africa.

high-end 最高級の

Antananarivo アンタナナリボ（マダガスカルの首都）

Madagascar マダガスカル（Republic of Madagascar）

Lalaina Ravelomanana: I like mixing caviar with salmon because of its mellow, slightly fatty nature, which doesn't distort the taste of the caviar. [1]( ) ( ) ( ) ( ) ( ) ( ) ( )—perfect. I like ingredients which are not too strong, so the caviar is not affected.

Narrator: It's in this factory, 60 kilometers outside the capital, that the caviar is processed. After the cutting, weighing and rinsing, comes the all-important step of salting the caviar, a very delicate task.

Flavien Rakotosalama: You really have to respect the 60-second time limit—if not, the caviar becomes soft [2]( ) ( ) ( ) ( ) ( ) ( ). If you go over a minute you might completely ruin the eggs.

Narrator: This Madagascan caviar is sold for 750 euros per kilo, [3]( ) ( ) ( ) ( ) ( ) ( ) its French equivalent. But the producers say that this doesn't impact the quality.

Georges Andrianjatovo: You can see it's got a nice gray color. When I smell it, I'm getting fresh butter. And when I taste it, [4]( ) ( ) ( ) ( ) ( ) ( ). I think it's good caviar.

Narrator: The sturgeon fish, imported in fertilized egg form from Russia, are kept in carefully monitored conditions in Lake Mantasoa, perched high up at 1,400 meters above sea level.

sturgeon fish チョウザメ

Lake Mantasoa マンタソア湖

Delphyne Dabezies: Our lake has very, very pure water, fed only by rainwater and with no industrial or commercial activities in the surrounding area. We also produce fish food, with fresh products from Madagascar, all natural. So ⁵(   ) (   ) (   ) (   ) (   ).

Narrator: At the moment, Madagascan caviar production represents a drop in the ocean, with only one tonne produced last year in a world market of 340 tonnes. But the entrepreneurs behind the project are ambitious and hope to expand fivefold this year.

fivefold 5倍に

4 COMPREHENSION CHECK | *Second Viewing*

WEB動画 DVD

▷▷ *Watch the news clip again and answer the following questions in English.*

1. What does the chef Ravelomanana take advantage of?
   ....

2. How is the caviar processed in the factory?
   ....

3. Why is the caviar processed within 60 seconds?
   ....

4. In what form are the sturgeon fish imported from Russia?
   ....

5. How many tons of caviar did Madagascar produce last year?
   ....

5 SUMMARY

CD 2-19

▷▷ *Listen to the recording and complete the summary.*

Locally renowned chef Lalaina Ravelomanana is creating new recipes to take advantage of Madagascar's own caviar. Madagascan caviar is sold for 750 euros per kilo, two to three times ¹(   ) than its French equivalent. Madagascan caviar

89

$^2($ $)$ was only one tonne last year in a world market of 340 tonnes. But the entrepreneurs behind the project are $^3($ $)$ and hope to expand fivefold this year.

◤▌ READING

🎧 2-20

In all societies, local foods develop according to the conditions and ingredients within a particular region. Foods prepared locally and
5 passed down through generations often provoke deep emotions. Links between the place, the food, and the people create a strong identity. Eating food with others is much
10 more than just the act of eating. In Japan, for example, the seasons and prefectures are strongly associated with the food consumed. Food is a vital part of the culture. Nowadays, producers have more opportunity to break with old traditions. In a competitive industry,
15 where consumers are spoilt for choice, producers are always mindful of innovating, expanding, and maintaining their foods' popularity.

However, it is not easy to break the bonds between traditional food and the people who eat it. Studies show that the public quickly accepts changes in a product's packaging or processing. But they are less likely to accept direct modifications.
20 Researchers found that consumers enjoy products that seem authentic. There is less acceptance for food that changes essential ingredients, flavors, or tastes.

The result is that innovations are more likely found in food production or marketing than in the food itself. There are some exceptions to this. In recent years, for example, attitudes to eating farm products have changed. Many people are
25 turning away from meat, eggs, and milk, and are choosing alternatives. This change has resulted in the use of substitutes in a wide variety of dishes. There is also the growing attraction of fast food that has altered many people's daily eating habits.

Although there is a place for innovation, the research suggests nothing will change the attachment many people have for the food they have always enjoyed.

(280 words)

1 VOCABULARY CHECK

⊳ *Fill in the blanks with the most appropriate word from the list below.*

1. Getting enough nutrition is (　　　　　) for a healthy lifestyle.
2. The chef knows all the necessary (　　　　　) for the complicated dish by heart.
3. We can (　　　　　) sugar with maple syrup to cut down on calories.
4. There are many communally owned cats in this (　　　　　) area of the town.
5. The program is likely to work fine with some (　　　　　).

> ingredients modifications vital particular substitute

2 COMPREHENSION QUESTIONS

⊳ *Answer the following questions in English.*

1. Why do local foods provoke deep emotions?

   ....

2. What has a strong association with the food consumed in Japan?

   ....

3. What are producers mindful of in a competitive industry?

   ....

4. What changes does the public quickly accept?

   ....

5. What has altered many people's daily eating habits?

   ....

3 GRAMMAR CHECK

⊳ *Unscramble the following words and complete the sentences.*

1. The restaurant is planning [a, is, at, to, good, cook, hire, who] baking cakes.

   The restaurant is planning .... baking cakes.

2. Mark decided to [the, the, to, according, classify, color, pictures, prominent].

   Mark decided to ....

3. Alex often makes cheese from milk at home [time-consuming, pretty, although, be, it, can].

   Alex often makes cheese from milk at home ....
   ....

Traditional vs Innovative: Food culture you prefer

There are many cuisines classified as fusion.

▷▷ インターネットなどを利用し、さまざまなフュージョン料理について調べましょう。フュージョン料理の良い点ばかりでなく、伝統料理への影響など悪い点についても検討し、下記のどちらの意見を支持するか、主張、理由など自らの考えをまとめ、発表しましょう。

Which opinion do you support and why?

A *I would like to preserve traditional food culture.*

B *I would prefer to create innovative food.*

自分の意見 _____

理由

_____

_____

_____

REFERENCES	
A	**B**
伝統的な食文化	**フュージョン料理**
日本料理（和食）は、日本の風土と社会で発達した料理をいう。食品本来の味を利用し、旬などの季節感を大切にする特徴がある。和食は 2013 年にユネスコ無形文化遺産に登録された。	フュージョン料理は、さまざまな国、地域、または文化に由来するさまざまな料理の伝統の要素を組み合わせた料理である。このタイプの料理は、特定の料理スタイルに分類されることはなく、1970 年代以降、多くの現代的なレストラン料理の革新に貢献してきた。

Climate Change vs Natural Cycle: Is Earth really warming?

一般的には地球は温暖化していると考えられていて、気候変動への警告が発せられています。一方では、気温の変化は地球の自然なサイクルであり、警戒する必要はないという議論をする人もいます。皆さんはどう考えますか。

I LISTENING

1 KEY WORD STUDY | *Before Watching the Video*

▷▷ *Match each word with its definition.*

1. arctic ( )　　2. complexity ( )　　3. glacier ( )
4. iceberg ( )　　5. interact ( )　　6. melt ( )
7. prediction ( )　8. probe ( )　　9. transmit ( )
10. vintage ( )

> a. 探針　　b. 氷河　c. 古い　　d. 複雑さ、複雑なもの
> e. 送信する　f. 氷山　g. 溶ける　h. 北極の
> i. 相互に影響する　j. 予想

2 LISTENING PRACTICE 1 | *First Viewing*　　(Time 02:33) 📺 💿

▷▷ *Watch the news clip and write T if the statement is true or F if it is false.*

1. Greenland is warming twice as fast as the rest of the world. ( )
2. The ice in Greenland is melting only from the air warming. ( )
3. The probes transmit data about the temperature and salinity of the water. ( )
4. How ocean temperature variations will affect the Greenland ice sheet in the future is a big concern. ( )
5. Keeping the mission in the air is easy in eastern Greenland with accessible communications and transport. ( )

3 LISTENING PRACTICE 2

⊳⊳ *Listen to the recording and fill in the missing words.*

WEB動画 DVD CD 2-22

Narrator: Eighty-five percent of Greenland is covered in ice, putting this vast territory on the front line of melting Arctic ice in a region that is warming twice as fast as the rest of the planet. From this remote airfield, NASA scientists are taking to the skies, to gather data to better understand ¹( ) ( ) ( ) ( ) ( ) how oceans interact with glaciers and contribute to melting them.

Greenland グリーンランド

Joshua Willis: Well, of course, the planet is heating up because of human-caused climate change. And Greenland is feeling the impact in a big way. Now a lot of people think of the ice here ²( ) ( ) ( ) ( ) ( ) ( ), sort of like an ice cube under a hair dryer, but in fact the oceans are also eating away at the ice's edges. That's because the glaciers flow right into the ocean and they can feel the warming water and are retreating because of it.

Narrator: Oceans Melting Greenland, or OMG, has been flying these missions since 2015. Flying over fjords, glaciers, and icebergs in a vintage, World War 2-era plane, they drop probes into the water below to measure the temperature of the Arctic. At the signal, the crew drops the probe into the water below, ³( ) ( ) ( ) ( ) ( ) ( ). Once they hit the ocean, they start transmitting data about the temperature and salinity of the water down to the seabed. The data is radioed back to the plane and can be compared against data from flights in the winter to see how warm water from the oceans is affecting

Oceans Melting Greenland (OMG) グリーンランドの氷河の融解に対する海洋の影響を調査するNASAのミッション
fjord フィヨルド、峡江
World War 2 第二次世界大戦

salinity 塩分濃度

glaciers.

Ian Fenty: It's a major open question, how ocean temperature variations will affect the Greenland ice sheet in the future, and so the data we're

collecting are super valuable because they're allowing us for the very first time to quantitatively relate ocean temperature changes with the melting of the ice sheet.

quantitatively 量的に、定量的に

Narrator: But in remote eastern Greenland, [4]( ) ( ) ( ) ( ) ( ), even keeping the mission in the air is a challenge.

Ian McCubbin: The complexities of dealing with Greenland's remoteness is a unique challenge [5]( ) ( ) ( ) ( ) ( ) in a way I never thought I could have excitement.

Narrator: Flying dozens of flights and dropping hundreds of probes over five years, OMG's aim is to see how much the oceans are melting these glaciers, something these scientists hope will improve predictions of sea-level rise, as Greenland's ice vanishes.

---

4 COMPREHENSION CHECK | *Second Viewing*

WEB動画 DVD

▷▷ *Watch the news clip again and answer the following questions in English.*

1. What percentage of Greenland is covered in ice?

   ....

2. Why does Joshua Wills think the Earth is heating up?

   ....

3. What does OMG measure by dropping probes into the water?

   ....

4. What does Ian McCubbin think is a unique challenge?

   ....

5. What is OMG's aim by dropping probes from a plane?

   ....

5 | SUMMARY

▷▷ *Listen to the recording and complete the summary.*

Eighty-five percent of Greenland is covered in ice, putting this vast territory on the front line of melting Arctic ice in a region that is warming ¹(   ) as fast as the rest of the planet. A lot of people think of the ice here as melting from the air warming, like an ice cube under a hair dryer, but in fact the oceans are also eating away at the ice's edges. It's a major open question how ocean temperature ²(   ) will affect the Greenland ice sheet in the future, and so the data being collected are very valuable because they make it possible for the first time to ³(   ) relate ocean temperature changes with the melting of the ice sheet.

▌ READING

The weather patterns of the Earth change continuously. The reasons for this include small shifts of the Earth's center that vary the focus of sunlight, volcanic eruptions that leave reflective particles in the air, and changes in the sun's power. As a result, the levels of greenhouse gases in the atmosphere have always varied,

5 surface temperatures have heated and cooled, and sea levels have risen and fallen. However, research suggests that current changes in climate are not part of the normal processes. It ascribes the situation to global warming.

Scientists argue that the rapid warming of the Earth is a result of burning fossil fuels. They cite data that attests to the considerable rise in temperatures since the

10 early 20th century. Small, steady changes have become sharp increases in the last 50 years. This rise results in melting ice caps, longer seasons, and changing rainfall patterns. However, the use of coal, oil, and gas is not the only problem. Cutting down sizeable carbon-absorbing forest areas is also a concern as it increases gas levels in the atmosphere.

15 Despite this, several scientists argue that climate change is not related to fossil fuels. High carbon dioxide levels are not responsible for the temperature rise, they say. They insist that rising temperatures are beyond our control, and that heating fluctuates with the sun and is part of a natural process. They blame the media, politicians, and a climate "industry" for misleading the public.

20 It is clear that climate changes are continuous, but it is difficult to ignore the steep rises confirmed by the data, nor the human effect on the environment. Without a collective effort, it will be a challenge to prevent further warming.

(281 words)

▌NOTES

reflective 反射する　**sizeable** かなりの

1 VOCABULARY CHECK

▷▷ *Fill in the blanks with the most appropriate word from the list below.*

1. Cindy (   ) her success to luck rather than her efforts.
2. Sponges can (   ) a surprising amount of water.
3. The stock market tends to (   ) in response to economic policies.
4. The report (   ) the discovery of a new species of butterfly.
5. The lawyer (   ) that her client was not involved in the crime.

attested   ascribed   absorb   confirmed   fluctuate

2 COMPREHENSION QUESTIONS

▷▷ *Answer the following questions in English.*

1. What are the reasons for the change in the weather patterns of the Earth?

   ....

2. What do many scientists think has caused the rapid warming of the Earth?

   ....

3. What has the considerable rise in temperatures caused?

   ....

4. What do those who think climate change is not related to fossil fuels say about

   carbon dioxide levels?

   ....

5. Who do they blame for misleading the public?

   ....

3 GRAMMAR CHECK

▷▷ *Unscramble the following words and complete the sentences.*

1. It has been [since, this, raining, and, morning, off, on].

   It has been ....

2. The stay-home period was partly [the, the, responsible, number, increase, in, for]
   of household pets.

   The stay-home period was partly ....
    of household pets.

3. The rugby team won the championship [practice, lack, of, its, despite] last year.

   The rugby team won the championship .... last year.

97

Climate Change vs Natural Cycle: Is Earth really warming?

There are many opinions about global warming.

▷ インターネットなどを利用し、地球温暖化について調べましょう。温暖化を肯定し、防止策を推奨する意見ばかりでなく、自然のサイクルであるというような否定的な意見についても検討し、下記のどちらの意見を支持するか、主張、理由など自らの考えをまとめ、発表しましょう。

Which opinion do you support and why?

A *Climate change and global warming have become severe, and we need to do something to prevent them.*

B *The Earth is becoming a little warmer, but it is a natural cycle. There have always been certain periods of temperature changes in history.*

自分の意見 _____

理由

_____

_____

REFERENCES

A

地球温暖化

現在の地球は過去 1400 年で最も暖かくなっている。この地球規模で気温や海水温が上昇し氷河や氷床が縮小する現象、すなわち地球温暖化は、平均的な気温の上昇のみならず、異常高温（熱波）や大雨・干ばつの増加などのさまざまな気候の変化をともなっている。その影響は、早い春の訪れなどによる生物活動の変化や、水資源や農作物への影響など、自然生態系や人間社会にすでに現れている。将来、地球の気温はさらに上昇すると予想され、水、生態系、食糧、沿岸域、健康などでより深刻な影響が生じると考えられている。国土交通省気象庁「地球温暖化とは」(https://www.data.jma.go.jp/cpdinfo/chishiki_ondanka/p01.html)

B

『地球温暖化懐疑論と環境情報』伊藤朋恭

社会情報学研究 (16), 149-159, 2007, 大妻女子大学

化石燃料から排出される二酸化炭素が地球温暖化を引き起こしていることはすでに通説として定着している。確かに大局的に見れば温暖化に向かっており、少なくてもその一因が人為的二酸化炭素の排出にあることは確かであろうし、将来に備える予防的見地から対策を考えることは合理的である。しかし一方では人為的温暖化という通説を疑問視する見方も多く存在しており、その中には合理的な意見も少なくない。本稿ではこれらの懐疑的意見を 5 つに大別して整理することを試みた。懐疑論の中で最も中心的な意見は、温暖化に寄与している大きな要因は人為的なものではなく、太陽活動の変動などの自然現象にあるとするものである。

LESSON 15

Natural vs Artificial: Rewilding and gardening

手入れの整った庭園は見た目には美しいですが、環境への影響はないのでしょうか。手つかずの自然と人工的に整備された自然では、どちらが地球にやさしいのでしょうか。

I LISTENING

1 KEY WORD STUDY | *Before Watching the Video*

▷▷ *Match each word with its definition.*

1. adhere ( )	2. fauna ( )	3. futile ( )
4. habitat ( )	5. haven ( )	6. messy ( )
7. proponent ( )	8. thrive ( )	9. vacant ( )
10. vacate ( )		

a. 立ち退く   b. 無駄な、効果のない   c. 固執する   d. 空の
e. 取り散らかした   f. 動物区系   g. 避難所、安息所   h. 支持者
i. 生息地、居住環境   j. 生い茂る

2 LISTENING PRACTICE 1 | *First Viewing*   (Time 02:57)

▷▷ *Watch the news clip and write T if the statement is true or F if it is false.*

1. Typical gardens in American suburbs have lawns and flower boxes. ( )
2. Anna Burger's gardens and that of her neighbor have earned certifications. ( )
3. Professor Chris Swan and his students have turned vacant lots in Baltimore into beautifully planned gardens. ( )
4. According to a recent study, replacing lots with greenery can lead to an increase in crime. ( )
5. Supporters of neat and tidy gardens have encouraged the project. ( )

99

 2-26

▷▷ *Listen to the recording and fill in the missing words.*

Narrator: Nestled among the bustling streets of Washington, DC, sits this oasis of overgrown plants—a haven for local species and wildlife. Anna Burger's landscaping style  is known as "rewilding"—or returning one's garden back to a more natural state in lieu of the manicured lawns and flower boxes typical of many American suburbs.

in lieu of 〜の代わりに
manicure 刈り込む

Anna Burger: We had read about it. We also knew that putting chemicals on grass to try to keep it green seemed to be a futile process that wasn't good for kids playing on it or the environment or anything else. We really wanted to try to [1]( ) ( ) ( ) ( ) ( ) ( ) ( ) that was in a sense easy to take care of but also native plants, things that grew in this area.

Narrator: This Bohemian style is more than just a look. Both Anna and her neighbor Jim's gardens have earned National Wildlife Habitat certifications for providing a space with food, water, and shelter for local fauna.

National Wildlife Habitat certification 野生生物生息地証明

Jim Nichols: I was interested in trying to create a space that took care of the animals in the neighborhood. So, I try to keep places for the birds to nest, especially in the winter or you  know [2]( ) ( ) ( ) ( ) ( ). And I also keep a lot of bird baths and stuff and I try to keep them clean so that there's places for the animals to feed.

Narrator: Some 30 miles north in Baltimore, [3]( ) ( ) ( ) ( ) ( ) ( ).

100

Chris Swan: This is where two row homes once stood okay. All of these homes are vacated, so there are roughly 14,000 of these and 17,000 of those and they all have to come down. But then what to do with the land?

Narrator: Professor Chris Swan and a group of his students have turned dozens of vacant lots in Baltimore into thriving gardens like this one, [4]( ) ( ) ( ) ( ). A recent study found that replacing lots with greenery can lead to a reduction in crime and improved mental health in addition to the environmental benefits it provides.

Chris Swan: More biodiversity of plants, we know it contributes to more biodiversity of insects, which can lead to more biodiversity of larger animals, birds probably being the most interesting. The other part of that is that that often looks messy, it looks unkempt, and people tend to still adhere to [5]( ) ( ) ( ) ( ) ( ) ( ).

biodiversity 生物多様性

unkempt 乱れた

Narrator: Pushback from some neat and tidy garden proponents has brought the project to a halt. But as people think of new ways to combat climate change, rewilding is beginning to take root as a global movement.

▷▷ *Watch the news clip again and answer the following questions in English.*

1. What does the word rewilding mean?

....

2. What does Anna Burger think is not good for kids?

....

3. What was Jim Nichols interested in trying to create?

....

4. What happened to the two row homes?

....

5. What can more biodiversity of plants lead to?

....

5 SUMMARY 2-27

▷▷ *Listen to the recording and complete the summary.*

Anna Burger's landscaping style is known as "rewilding"—or returning one's garden to a more natural state in lieu of the manicured lawns and flower boxes typical of many American [1]( ). Both Anna and her neighbor Jim's gardens have earned National Wildlife Habitat certifications for providing a space with food, water, and shelter for local fauna. Professor Chris Swan and a group of his students have turned dozens of [2]( ) lots in Baltimore into thriving gardens, using mostly native species. They know more biodiversity of plants [3]( ) to more biodiversity of insects, and can lead to more biodiversity of larger animals, birds probably being the most interesting.

❙❙ READING 2-28

Over the centuries, humans have gradually expanded their territory. As towns and farms grow, they absorb large areas of land. By using the land, human activity upsets the wildlife that lives there. As a result, it destroys the balance of nature and provokes a loss of biodiversity. Rewilding is a method of restoring the natural
5 ecosystem and returning the land to nature.

Many agree that done well; rewilding can restore areas impacted by development. Some believe it is a duty to preserve species that human activities 10 have reduced. If the ecosystem can be re-established, it may help mitigate the effects of climate change. Rewilding, then, has several benefits. It is thought that re-introducing plants will increase 15 the number of insects and animals that

feed on them. Furthermore, rewilding prevents natural disasters such as floods or fires. Re-planted trees grow roots that allow water to drain deep into the ground. Animals eat the vegetation from areas at risk from wildfires. Finally, allowing sites to grow naturally will enable people to enjoy the wildlife that returns to new habitats.

20 Others, however, argue that there could be unintended consequences without knowing how all the systems work together. They believe that if there is no check on re-introduced animals, all the species in the area would be in danger. In addition, it is unclear how different species might react to each other. Re-introducing a new species may further upset the balance of the land. Furthermore, farmers worry that newly 25 introduced predators would threaten and kill livestock.

There are limitations to how much rewilding can restore a damaged ecosystem. However, there are evident benefits to using natural methods to rebuild biodiversity.

(276 words)

NOTES

mitigate 軽減する **livestock** 家畜

1 VOCABULARY CHECK

▷▷ *Fill in the blanks with the most appropriate word from the list below.*

1. The sparse (   ) of Antarctica is very different from that of Japan.
2. It is sometimes difficult to predict the (   ) of action at the beginning.
3. Wild animals often fight to protect their (   ).
4. The construction plan was modified so as not to (   ) the habitats of koalas.
5. It took nearly 10 years to (   ) the palace to its former glory.

territory   consequences   vegetation   threaten   restore

2 COMPREHENSION QUESTIONS

▷▷ *Answer the following questions in English.*

1. What is lost when the balance of nature is destroyed?

   ....

2. What do supporters of rewilding believe is a duty of human beings?

   ....

3. What will a re-introduction of plants increase?

   ....

4. What are examples of natural disasters rewilding can prevent?

   ....

5. Why are some people against the re-introduction of new species?

   ....

3 GRAMMAR CHECK

▷▷ *Unscramble the following words and complete the sentences.*

1. You should sometimes rest your eyes [at, in, by, distance, something, looking, the].

   You should sometimes rest your eyes ....

   ....

2. Virtual sightseeing enables you [going, enjoy, cultures, to, without, abroad, different].

   Virtual sightseeing enables you ....

   ....

3. [would, you, if, in, could, appreciate, fill, it, I] this survey on national parks.

   .... this survey on national parks.

DISCUSSION

Natural vs Artificial: Rewilding and gardening

Which style of garden do you think is better?

▷ インターネットなどを利用し、自然農法、フォーマルガーデンについて調べましょう。自然農法、フォーマルガーデンのそれぞれの良い点、悪い点について検討し、下記のどちらの意見を支持するか、主張、理由など自らの考えをまとめ、発表しましょう。

Which opinion do you support and why?

◤A *Keeping nature as it is, is a better method for agriculture and gardening, and the use of chemicals should be prohibited.*

◤B *Humans should take care of nature. French and English gardens are attractive, and using pesticides and chemicals to keep gardens neat is necessary.*

自分の意見 ＿＿＿＿＿

理由

＿＿＿＿＿＿＿＿＿＿＿＿＿＿＿＿＿＿＿
＿＿＿＿＿＿＿＿＿＿＿＿＿＿＿＿＿＿＿
＿＿＿＿＿＿＿＿＿＿＿＿＿＿＿＿＿＿＿

REFERENCES

A	B
自然農法 自然農法の理念：大自然を尊重し、その摂理を規範に順応する。 自然農法の原理：生きている土の偉大な能力を発揮させる。 生命を生かし、より豊かにしようとする自然の働きを引き出し、永続的な生産を行うことが自然農法の目標である。 公益財団法人自然農法国際研究開発センター「自然農法とは」http://www.infrc.or.jp/about/	**ガーデニング** ヨーロッパのガーデニングには、大きく分けて、フランスの「フレンチガーデン（フランス式庭園）」とイギリスの「ブリティッシュガーデン（イギリス式庭園）」の2つの様式がある。 フランス式は、幾何学的に植物が配置された形の整った庭で、イギリス式は、田舎の自然な雰囲気になるよう、あえて無造作に植物を配置した庭である。

Archaeology vs Treasure Hunting: Who owns wreckage?

沈没船の財宝はだれのものでしょうか。考古学調査と宝探しでは、優先されるべきはどちらでしょうか。歴史的な価値のあるものから過去を知り、後世へ伝えることと、お金儲けでは、どちらを選びますか。

I LISTENING

1 KEY WORD STUDY | *Before Watching the Video*

▷▷ *Match each word with its definition.*

1. archaeologist ( )　　2. coastline　　( )　　3. loaded　　( )

4. loot　　( )　　5. pottery　　( )　　6. shipwreck　　( )

7. tackle　　( )　　8. timber　　( )　　9. unauthorized ( )

10. underwater　( )

a. 難破船	b. 盗む	c. 陶器	d. 材木
e. 権限のない	f. 水中の	g. 海岸線	h. 荷を積んだ
i. 考古学者	j. 取り組む		

2 LISTENING PRACTICE 1 | *First Viewing*   (Time 02:49) 📺 💿 DVD

▷▷ *Watch the news clip and write T if the statement is true or F if it is false.*

1. The marine archaeologists dived into a 500-year-old wreck of merchant ship.

   ( )

2. Important pottery was lost from the shipwreck in storms.　　　　( )

3. The marine archaeologists think artifacts are more valuable if they are kept in the Maritime Museum.　　　　( )

4. Unauthorized dive boats are monitored by the coastguard, navy, and police.

   ( )

5. Divers need to learn new skills to move around the wrecks without causing damage.　　　　( )

3 LISTENING PRACTICE 2

WEB動画 📺 | 💿 DVD | 💿 CD | 2-30

▷▷ *Listen to the recording and fill in the missing words.*

Narrator: On the Baltic waters of the Stockholm archipelago, these marine archaeologists make their final preparations to dive. Their destination: a 500-year-old merchant ship that sank here, loaded with cargo. When the team discovered the wreck in 2017, they realized [1]( ) ( ) ( ) ( ) ( ) had huge historic value. But returning to this site just months later, they found key artifacts had been stolen.

Baltic バルト海の

Jim Hansson: We saw that somebody has found this position and stolen this important pottery, so I was really angry, I was cursing in my full-face mask [2]( ) ( ) ( ) ( ) ( ), and so pissed off and really angry. It's so unnecessary.

Narrator: Wrecks like this dot Sweden's eastern coastline—the timber is well preserved because of the Baltic's low salt content. But the team say they've noticed several other thefts from shipwrecks in this area. For archaeologist Jim Hansson, items like this cooking pot [3]( ) ( ) ( ) ( ) ( ) ( ) ship are of more value when they are left in place on the wreckage. He says others like it must be protected.

Jim Hansson: If everything is still there at the wreck, we can tell a story as close to reality as possible, because [4]( ) ( ) ( ) ( ), ( ), ( ) whatsoever on these kind of things, so we need these artifacts.

Narrator: To tackle the problem, Hansson and his colleagues at Sweden's Maritime Museum have launched a project to photograph and film the sites. They hope the information they gather underwater will allow them to protect them.

Maritime Museum 海事博物館

Patrik Hoglund: We can come back and check with the photos and check with those stations and on the survey plan what happens—if people have been here looting or if natural causes have made the wreck fall apart.

Narrator: The coastguard, navy, and police have agreed to monitor for unauthorized dive boats. And coastguard divers like these are being trained by the Maritime Museum's team to help monitor the wrecks. Documenting sensitive historic sites requires new skills for the divers, who have to learn to move around them without causing damage and to note key details.

Patrik Dahlgren: This is very different for us, but we understand the value, it feels meaningful and we know that [5]( ) ( ) ( ) ( ) on these shipwrecks, and we feel that we need to have control and know what's going on on these wrecks.

Narrator: With the authorities on board to help, these archaeologists hope to be able to better protect the Baltic's underwater history and preserve the wrecks beneath the waves for future generations to learn from.

4 COMPREHENSION CHECK | *Second Viewing*

▷▷ *Watch the news clip again and answer the following questions in English.*

1. What did the marine archaeologists find after returning to the shipwreck months later?

    ....

2. Why is the timber well preserved off Sweden's eastern coastline?

    ....

3. What can the marine archaeologists tell if things are not stolen from the shripwrecks?

    ....

4. Why have Jim Hasson and his colleagues launched a project to photograph and film the shipwreck sites?

    ....

5. What do the archaeologists hope to achieve with the cooperation of the authorities?

    ....

5 SUMMARY

 2-31

▷▷ *Listen to the recording and complete the summary.*

When the team of marine archaeologists discovered the wreck in 2017, they realized the goods [1]( ) on its deck had huge historic value. But returning to this site just months later, they found key artifacts had been [2]( ). With the authorities on board to help, these archaeologists hope to be able to better protect the Baltic's underwater history and preserve the wrecks [3]( ) the waves for future generations to learn from.

▌ READING

 2-32

Two centuries ago, Lord Elgin took the "Parthenon Frieze" sculptures from Greece to Britain. The collection is famously known as the "Elgin Marbles". Although many have called for their return to Greece, the trustees of the British Museum have refused, and they remain there. The marbles are among thousands of cultural
5   artifacts removed in disputed circumstances.

Museums across the world have collected art pieces for hundreds of years. Collectors have often taken pieces from countries during times of conflict or colonial rule. Some museums have thousands of items but only display a selected few. In recent times, critics have argued that museums should return the artworks.

Firstly, they argue that the artifacts belong to the people of the countries they were taken from. They say it is morally wrong to keep objects taken at a time of turmoil or repression. Furthermore, they say that the artifacts are culturally significant and have no real meaning for people of other countries. They also maintain that many objects are put in storage and rarely seen. Finally, they claim that collections are constantly moving, and there is no longer a need for museums to "own" pieces.

The museums defend their decision to keep many of the artifacts. They say that if they return some items, there would be constant requests for other pieces. Returning items would cause a crisis for museums. They say that storing pieces protects them, and other countries may not have the preservation resources. They point to the artworks already deteriorated, stolen, or deliberately destroyed. Finally, they say the artworks are universal and more people gain access to them in major museums.

There are solid arguments for and against returning objects to their native countries. However, which items to return must be weighed against the need for preservation.

(279 words)

NOTES

trustee 理事   **turmoil** 混乱   **repression** 抑圧

1 | VOCABULARY CHECK

▷▷ *Fill in the blanks with the most appropriate word from the list below.*

1. The museum had to change its opening hours under the current (   ).
2. Fragile artifacts can (   ) easily if not handled with care.
3. It is a delicate process to (   ) dust from historical relics.
4. Controlling the temperature and humidity of the storage is necessary for the (   ) of old documents.
5. Museums in Britain have artifacts from around the world partly as a result of British (   ) power in the past.

> remove   circumstances   colonial   preservation   deteriorate

2 COMPREHENSION QUESTIONS

▷ *Answer the following questions in English.*

1. From where did Lord Elgin take the "Parthenon Frieze" sculptures?

   ....

2. Why have critics argued that museums should return artworks?

   ....

3. Why do critics think that museums no longer need to "own" art pieces?

   ....

4. Why do museums think that returning items would cause a crisis?

   ....

5. What do museums say about keeping artworks in major museums?

   ....

3 GRAMMAR CHECK

▷ *Unscramble the following words and complete the sentences.*

1. [stadium, people, thousands, at, the, gathered, of] to watch the final round of the tournament.

   .... to watch the final round of the tournament.

2. Jamie was [compete, qualified, the, who, athletes, to, among] in the Olympics.

   Jamie was .... in the Olympics.

3. The special exhibition is [at, museum, no, national, held, the, longer].

   The special exhibition is ....

Archaeology vs Treasure Hunting: Who owns wreckage?

Have you dreamed of becoming rich by finding abandoned treasure?

▷ インターネットなどを利用し、宝探しと文化財保護について調べましょう。トレジャーハントの可能性や一攫千金など良い点ばかりでなく、法規制や文化財保護などの観点からも検討し、下記のどちらの意見を支持するか、主張、理由など自らの考えをまとめ、発表しましょう。

Which opinion do you support and why?

> **A** *Archaeology is an important study, and so the shipwrecks and artifacts should be protected from treasure hunters because of their historical value.*

> **B** *Shipwrecks are available for anyone, and it is good for treasure hunters to freely obtain artifacts.*

自分の意見 ＿＿＿＿＿＿

理由

＿＿＿＿＿＿＿＿＿＿＿＿＿＿＿＿＿＿＿＿＿＿＿＿＿＿＿＿＿＿＿＿＿

＿＿＿＿＿＿＿＿＿＿＿＿＿＿＿＿＿＿＿＿＿＿＿＿＿＿＿＿＿＿＿＿＿

＿＿＿＿＿＿＿＿＿＿＿＿＿＿＿＿＿＿＿＿＿＿＿＿＿＿＿＿＿＿＿＿＿

REFERENCES

A	**B**
文化財保護協力の必要性 文化財は、様々な人々と諸民族の国々とが交渉し合って形成された世界の長い歴史の中で生まれ、今日に伝えられてきた人類の貴重な財産である。それは、世界の国々の歴史や文化的伝統の理解に欠くことができないものであると同時に、世界の国々の文化の発展の基礎をなすものである。 文化庁 https://www.bunka.go.jp/seisaku/bunkazai/hokoku/kokusai/hitsuyosei.html	**民法第 241 条　埋蔵物の発見** 埋蔵物は、遺失物法の定めるところに従い公告をした後六箇月以内にその所有者が判明しないときは、これを発見した者がその所有権を取得する。ただし、他人の所有する物の中から発見された埋蔵物については、これを発見した者及びその他人が等しい割合でその所有権を取得する。

Web動画のご案内 **StreamLine**

本テキストの映像は、オンラインでのストリーミング再生になります。下記URLよりご利用ください。なお**有効期限は、はじめてログインした時点から1年半**です。

http://st.seibido.co.jp

① ログイン画面

🔒 **LOGIN**

テキストに添付されているシールをはがして、
12桁のアクセスコードをご入力ください。

[　　] - [　　] - [　　]

同意してログイン

以下の「利用規約」をご確認頂き、同意する場合は
上記ボタン【同意してログイン】を押してください。

利用規約

1. このウェブサイト（以下「本サイト」といいます）は、
株式会社成美堂（以下「弊社」といいます）が運営しています。
弊社の商品・サービス（以下「本サービス」といいます）利用時の
会員登録の有無を問わず、本サイトの利用にあたっては、
以下のご利用条件をお読み頂き、これらの条件にご同意の上ご利用ください。

2. 本サービスに関して個別に利用規約がある場合、
本規約に加えそれらも適用されます。

3. 本サイトを通じて、弊社の商品を販売する第三者のウェブサイトに
ご案内ないしリンクされることがあります。
リンク先ウェブサイトにおいて提供された個人情報は

> 巻末に添付されているシールをはがして、アクセスコードをご入力ください。

② メニュー画面

AFP World Focus
−Environment, Health, and Technology−

アクセスコード有効期限：2018年4月30日

🎬 **Video**　　🎵 **Audio**

Lesson 1: Global Warming and Climat... ＞

Lesson 2: Diet and Health for Long ... ＞

Lesson 3: Self-Driving for the Futu... ＞

Lesson 4: Sustaining Biodiversity a... ＞

Lesson 5: 3D Printers for Creating ... ＞

Lesson 6: IT and Education ＞

Lesson 7: Protection from Natural D... ＞

Lesson 8: Practical Uses of Drones ... ＞

> 「Video」または「Audio」を選択すると、それぞれストリーミング再生ができます。

③ 再生画面

AFP World Focus
−Environment, Health, and Technology−

アクセスコード有効期限：2018年4月30日

▶

Lesson 2:
Diet and Health for Long Lives
食習慣：長生きのためのスーパーフードを探す

推奨動作環境

【PC OS】
Windows 7~　/　Mac 10.8~

【Mobile OS】
iOS / Android　※Androidの場合は4.x~が推奨

【Desktop ブラウザ】
Internet Explorer 9~ / Firefox / Chrome / Safari /
Microsoft Edge

TEXT PRODUCTION STAFF

edited by	編集
Minako Hagiwara	萩原 美奈子

cover design by	表紙デザイン
Ruben Frosali	ルーベン・フロサリ

text design by	本文デザイン
Ruben Frosali	ルーベン・フロサリ

CD PRODUCTION STAFF

recorded by	吹き込み者
Karen Haedrich (AmE)	カレン・ヘドリック (アメリカ英語)
Rachel Walzer (AmE)	レイチェル・ワルザー (アメリカ英語)
Howard Colefield (AmE)	ハワード・コールフィールド (アメリカ英語)
Dominic Allen (AmE)	ドミニク・アレン （アメリカ英語)

AFP World News Report 6
AFPニュースで見る世界 6

2022年1月20日　初版発行
2023年3月15日　第4刷発行

著　　者　宍戸 真
　　　　　Kevin Murphy
　　　　　高橋 真理子

発 行 者　佐野 英一郎

発 行 所　株式会社 成美堂
　　　　　〒101-0052　東京都千代田区神田小川町3-22
　　　　　TEL 03-3291-2261　FAX 03-3293-5490
　　　　　https://www.seibido.co.jp

印 刷・製 本　三美印刷株式会社

ISBN 978-4-7919-7250-0　　　　　　　　　　　　Printed in Japan